WORLD
HISTORY SERIES

The Making of the Atom Bomb

by
Victoria Sherrow

Lucent Books, P.O. Box 289011, San Diego, CA 92198-9011

Library of Congress Cataloging-in-Publication Data

Sherrow, Victoria.
    The making of the atom bomb / by Victoria Sherrow.
        p.   cm.—(World history series)
    Includes bibliographical references and index.
    Summary: Discusses various topics connected to the pro-
duction of the atom bomb, including the development of nu-
clear energy, work on atomic weapons at Los Alamos and
other sites, and the decision to use the first atomic bomb during World War II.
    ISBN 1-56006-585-0 (lib. : alk. paper)
    1. World War, 1939–1945—Aerial operations, American—
Juvenile literature. 2. Atomic bomb—New Mexico—Los
Alamos—History—Juvenile literature. 3. Nuclear weapons—
United States—History—Juvenile literature. 4. Deterrence
(Strategy)—United States—History—Juvenile literature. 5.
Hiroshima-shi (Japan)—History—Bombardment, 1945—Juve-
nile literature. 6. Nagasaki-shi (Japan)—History—Bombard-
ment, 1945—Juvenile literature. 7. Atomic bomb—History—
Juvenile literature. 8. United States—Military policy—Juve-
nile literature. [1. Atomic bomb—History.] I. Title. II. Series.

D790.S4954 2000
940.54'4973 21—dc21   99-042640

Cover photo: Physicist Ernest Lawrence adjusts one of
the cyclotrons used in the making of the atom bomb.

Contents

Foreword

Each year on the first day of school, nearly every history teacher faces the task of explaining why his or her students should study history. One logical answer to this question is that exploring what happened in our past explains how the things we often take for granted—our customs, ideas, and institutions—came to be. As statesman and historian Winston Churchill put it, "Every nation or group of nations has its own tale to tell. Knowledge of the trials and struggles is necessary to all who would comprehend the problems, perils, challenges, and opportunities which confront us today." Thus, a study of history puts modern ideas and institutions in perspective. For example, though the founders of the United States were talented and creative thinkers, they clearly did not invent the concept of democracy. Instead, they adapted some democratic ideas that had originated in ancient Greece and with which the Romans, the British, and others had experimented. An exploration of these cultures, then, reveals their very real connection to us through institutions that continue to shape our daily lives.

Another reason often given for studying history is the idea that lessons exist in the past from which contemporary societies can benefit and learn. This idea, although controversial, has always been an intriguing one for historians. Those who agree that society can benefit from the past often quote philosopher George Santayana's famous statement, "Those who cannot remember the past are condemned to repeat it." Historians who subscribe to Santayana's philosophy believe that, for example, studying the events that led up to the major world wars or other significant historical events would allow society to chart a different and more favorable course in the future.

Just as difficult as convincing students to realize the importance of studying history is the search for useful and interesting supplementary materials that present historical events in a context that can be easily understood. The volumes in Lucent Books' World History Series attempt to present a broad, balanced, and penetrating view of the march of history. Ancient Egypt's important wars and rulers, for example, are presented against the rich and colorful backdrop of Egyptian religious, social, and cultural developments. The series engages the reader by enhancing historical events with these cultural contexts. For example, in *Ancient Greece*, the text covers the role of women in that society. Slavery is discussed in *The Roman Empire*, as well as how slaves earned their freedom. The numerous and varied aspects of every-day life in these and other societies are explored in each volume of the series. Additionally, the series covers the major political, cultural, and philosophical ideas as the torch of civilization is passed from ancient Mesopotamia and Egypt, through Greece, Rome, Medieval Europe, and other world cultures, to the modern day.

The material in the series is formatted in a thorough, precise, and organized manner. Each volume offers the reader a comprehensive and clearly written overview of an important historical event or period. The topic under discussion is placed in a broad, historical context. For example, *The Italian Renaissance* begins with a discussion of the High Middle Ages and the loss of central control that allowed certain Italian cities to develop artistically. The book ends by looking forward to the Reformation and interpreting the societal changes that grew out of the Renaissance. Thus, students are not only involved in an historical era, but also enveloped by the events leading up to that era and the events following it.

One important and unique feature in the World History Series is the primary and secondary source quotations that richly supplement each volume. These quotes are useful in a number of ways. First, they allow students access to sources they would not normally be exposed to because of the difficulty and obscurity of the original source. The quotations range from interesting anecdotes to farsighted cultural perspectives and are drawn from historical witnesses both past and present. Second, the quotes demonstrate how and where historians themselves derive their information on the past as they strive to reach a consensus on historical events. Lastly, all of the quotes are footnoted, familiarizing students with the citation process and allowing them to verify quotes and/or look up the original source if the quote piques their interest.

Finally, the books in the World History Series provide a detailed launching point for further research. Each book contains a bibliography specifically geared toward student research. A second, annotated bibliography introduces students to all the sources the author consulted when compiling the book. A chronology of important dates gives students an overview, at a glance, of the topic covered. Where applicable, a glossary of terms is included.

In short, the series is designed not only to acquaint readers with the basics of history, but also to make them aware that their lives are a part of an ongoing human saga. Perhaps they will then come to the same realization as famed histor-ian Arnold Toynbee. In his monumental work, *A Study of History,* he wrote about becoming aware of history flowing through him in a mighty current, and of his own life "welling like a wave in the flow of this vast tide."

Important Dates in the Making of the Atom Bomb

1905
Albert Einstein develops his relativity theories and describes the relationship between mass and energy.

1938
In Germany, Otto Hahn, Fritz Strassman, and Lise Meitner split uranium atoms and detect the emergence of lighter elements; Enrico Fermi accepts Nobel Prize and moves to United States.

1940
American chemist Glenn Seaborg discovers plutonium; in May, Germany invades and occupies Belgium, the Netherlands, Norway, Denmark, and Luxembourg; in June, Germany invades and occupies France.

1900	1930	1935	1940	1943

1933
Adolf Hitler becomes chancellor of Germany; the Nazi government persecutes Jews and institutes harsh anti-Semitic laws.

1939
On October 11, President Franklin D. Roosevelt receives letter written by physicists Leo Szilard, Einstein, and Eugene Wigner about German atomic research; Roosevelt sets up secret committee to explore military implications.

1941
Japanese launch surprise air attack on U.S. naval base at Pearl Harbor on December 7; U.S. Congress declares war on Japan, Germany, and Italy on December 8.

1942
Fermi leads the S-1 group, which has been assigned to develop a nuclear pile a secret location at University of Chicago; in September, General Leslie Richard Groves of the U.S. Army Corps of Engineers is appointed military head of the Manhattan Project; on December 2 Fermi's S-1 group achieves first controlled nuclear reaction.

1943
Under General Groves and physicist Robert Oppenheimer, Project Y, the bomb-building project, is moved to a remote desert location in Los Alamos, New Mexico, on March 15; in November, the nuclear reactor at Oak Ridge, Tennessee, begins operating; plutonium plant operates in Hanford, Washington.

1944
In August, seventeen B-29s are taken to a plant in Omaha, Nebraska, to be modified for carrying atomic bombs; a group of servicemen, the 509th Composite Group, begins training for these missions under Colonel Paul C. Tibbets Jr.

January
On January 20, the first batch of U-235 is separated at Oak Ridge.

May
In May, the 509th is deployed to Tinian Island, its base of operations for the bombing missions.

| 1943 | 1944 | 1945 | Jan. | May | July | Aug. | Sept. |

July
Trinity test succeeds on July 16 when plutonium bomb is detonated near Alamogordo, about one hundred miles from Los Alamos; victorious Allies issue Potsdam Declaration on July 26 demanding an unconditional surrender from Japan; components of a uranium bomb are taken by sea to the airbase at Tinian Island.

August
B-29 *Enola Gay* drops uranium bomb on Hiroshima on August 6; B-29 *Bock's Car* drops plutonium bomb on Nagasaki on August 9.

September
On September 2, Japanese officially surrender to Supreme Allied Commander Douglas MacArthur aboard battleship *Missouri*.

Turbulent Times

Few events have affected the course of history as profoundly as the development of atomic weapons near the end of World War II. These devastating weapons, created in an atmosphere of intense fear that Nazi scientists would develop an atomic bomb first, catapulted the world into the nuclear age. Since the first atomic weapon was detonated in 1945, humankind has lived with the possibility of nuclear annihilation.

The scientific developments that paved the way for the atomic bomb unfolded over the course of decades as people

The development of the atom bomb near the end of World War II left an indelible mark on history. Humankind now lives in fear of this weapon's destructive power.

sought to understand more about the physical world. During those years, scientific discoveries were of interest mostly to scientists and teachers. By the time the crash development program known as the Manhattan Project began, however, interest in the nature of the atom had moved beyond the classroom and small laboratories and into the political arena. Atomic energy became the subject of intensive research and development for military purposes.

UNSETTLING TIMES

The decision to produce atomic weapons was made during a tumultuous and bloody era. Military aggression by Germany, Japan, and Italy had sparked a devastating world war that showed no signs of ending. Totalitarian governments backed by large, efficient armies threatened the security and freedom of nations around the world.

The 1920s and 1930s had set the stage for these events. In 1933 Adolf Hitler and his Nazis—National Socialists—gained control of the German government. Once in power, the Nazis persecuted Jews and others whom they labeled as inferior or enemies of the German state. Hitler claimed that Germany deserved more land, and his expanding armies invaded other countries to acquire it. In 1938 Nazi Germany annexed Austria and seized part of Czechoslovakia by force. Other European nations, hoping that Hitler would stop there, stood by without taking action.

Then, in September 1939, the Germans invaded Poland, where they set up a repressive occupation government and undertook a campaign to exterminate Poland's Jews, numbering about 3.3 million people. Polish intellectuals, Communists, and religious leaders were also targets of the newly installed German government. Finally awakening to the danger Hitler posed, England and France declared war on Germany. World War II, which would prove to be the most destructive conflict the world had ever seen, had begun.

Italy, under the leadership of Fascist dictator Benito Mussolini, joined Germany in its aggression. Mussolini built up the Italian military with plans to seize certain lands in the Middle East that were rich in resources. In 1935 Italian troops invaded Ethiopia. Although Mussolini did not share Hitler's racial ideology, he enforced anti-Semitic (anti-Jewish) policies in Italy to appease Hitler and cement his political ties to Germany.

While Europe was spiraling toward the chaos of war, political conflicts were also escalating in Asia. A military leader named Giichi Tanaka had become Japan's prime minister in 1927. He and other military leaders aggressively built up the army and navy. Because Japan lacked many natural resources of its own, the nation's leaders coveted lands in Southeast Asia that were rich in oil, tin, rubber, and other resources. In 1931 Japanese troops invaded Manchuria and proceeded to move south. In 1932, after invading Shanghai, Japanese forces moved on to other major Chinese cities, including Peking in 1937. Reports coming from

The Rise of Totalitarianism

During the 1920s and 1930s, a global depression caused widespread economic problems and unrest. In some countries, mainstream political leaders failed to devise programs that eased these problems, and they lost popular support.

In both Europe and Asia militarism, Fascism, and Communism attracted more followers. In Italy, Benito Mussolini and his militaristic Fascist Party came to power in 1922. By 1930 military leaders also dominated the Japanese government.

In Germany, Adolf Hitler's National Socialist (Nazi) Party, once regarded as a small extremist group, gained increasing support. The established political parties were disunited and the Nazis pitted one against the other. A forceful public speaker, Hitler vowed to strengthen the German economy and restore national pride, which had suffered after Germany's defeat in World War I. Seeing an opportunity to create scapegoats, Hitler blamed Germany's problems on Jews and Communists. By 1935 Hitler had become dictator of Germany, and the Nazis controlled nearly every aspect of life, including politics, the economy, the military, law enforcement, the judicial system, education, and the media.

Benito Mussolini (left), Adolf Hitler (right).

China indicated that the Japanese bombed civilian neighborhoods indiscriminately and committed brutal acts against Chinese civilians.

From Isolationist to Ally

Many Americans hoped that the United States would stay out of these escalating conflicts. Yet by September 1939 America's closest ally, Great Britain, was fighting Germany, which had attacked another of Britain's allies, Poland. The British prime minister, Winston Churchill, asked U.S. president Franklin D. Roosevelt for help. Although Roosevelt managed to send war materials to Britain, the mood in Congress and around the country opposed direct involvement in the fighting. By that time Congress had passed several measures designed to assure America's neutrality, and more than 90 percent of Americans believed U.S. policy should aim to stay out of foreign wars.

Many Americans who were living abroad had a different viewpoint. They observed firsthand the activities of dictators, military buildups, and broadening conflicts. Claude G. Bowers, the U.S. ambassador to Spain, watched civil war rage in that country, where antigovernment rebels led by General Francisco Franco were being aided by Nazi bombers and equipment. Bowers warned, "With every surrender [of an independent nation] the prospects of a European war grow darker."[1]

As the 1930s ended, Roosevelt was firmly convinced that the United States would not be able to remain neutral indefinitely. However, when the president mentioned this possibility in any of his public speeches, he found little support from either Congress or the public. He lamented, "It's a terrible thing to look over your shoulder when you are trying to lead—and to find no one there."[2]

By June 1940 Hitler had invaded several more European countries and seemed bent on world domination. But it was the Japanese, not the Germans, who finally forced the United States into the war. On December 7, 1941, the Japanese attacked the U.S. naval base at Pearl Harbor. In response, the United States declared war on Japan, while Germany declared war on the United States. The conflict was now truly global. Military forces fought each other with weapons that were unprecedented in their destructive power.

Japan's bombing of Pearl Harbor on December 7, 1941, roused the United States from its neutral position during the early days of World War II.

Cannon capable of hurling massive shells were developed by all sides; ships bristling with modern weapons cruised the oceans; and new, more powerful aircraft rained death on soldiers and civilians alike.

As the war raged, ever more terrifying weapons were developed. Now, for the first time, science had reached a point where it seemed possible to build atomic weapons. German scientists had split the atom in 1938, and Germany had gained access to uranium and other materials that were needed to build an atomic bomb. Foreign-born scientists who had fled from German-occupied Europe were horrified at the thought that the Nazis might create atomic weapons first, because whoever got these weapons first would very likely win the war.

A WEAPONS RACE

Led by Hungarian-born physicist Leo Szilard, expatriate scientists set out to warn

POLITICS OF APPEASEMENT

A forewarning of future trouble came in 1936, when Hitler sent troops into the Rhineland. The 1919 Treaty of Versailles, which ended World War I, made this region a buffer zone between Germany and France and military troops from both nations were banned from the area.

Nonetheless, the Germans secretly built barracks, roads, and rail lines in the Rhineland; on March 7, 1936, German troops openly marched into the area and set up army posts. Unaware that Hitler had ordered his troops to withdraw if they met resistance from French or British forces, which were better equipped than their own, neither France nor the country's allies moved against the Germans.

To avoid war, British and French leaders appeased Hitler and did not send troops to the Rhineland. Nor did they take action in 1938 when German troops seized the Sudetenland, a part of Czechoslovakia that bordered Germany. Hitler declared that the Sudetenland would be his last territorial claim in Europe.

Hoping to end German aggression, French and British leaders signed the Munich Pact, in which they agreed not to send troops to Czechoslovakia. After returning to London, British prime minister Neville Chamberlain was naively optimistic that the Munich agreement would result in a lasting peace.

Franklin Roosevelt (left) and Winston Churchill (right) were both aware of the dangers should the Nazis develop the atom bomb first.

President Roosevelt about the danger. At first, the president and military officials seemed unimpressed, but as scientists proceeded to split the uranium atom and then develop a controlled nuclear chain reaction, it became apparent to America's leaders that an atomic bomb was a real possibility. Roosevelt authorized research in the United States that steadily expanded between 1940 and 1945, when the first bombs were produced.

Work on the so-called Manhattan Project was arduous and required people to work fast and in the utmost secrecy. They had to generate new technologies to construct and test the bomb and its components. At every turn, they faced new questions: How could they gather the rare materials they needed? Was it possible to start and then control a nuclear chain reaction? What safety measures were needed at the laboratories? Where could bombs be built and tested? How would a bomb be encased, transported, and detonated? Despite incredible obstacles, those who worked on the project were convinced they must succeed, for if the Germans or Japanese produced these weapons first, they would be in a position to dominate the entire world.

Step by step, the people involved in the Manhattan Project moved closer to harnessing the secrets of atomic power—secrets that scientists sought yet dreaded. One era in human history was drawing to a close; a more perilous time was beginning.

1 "Energy That Does Not Come from the Sun"

Before the nineteenth century, scientists believed atoms were solid and indivisible. They regarded the atom as the smallest form of matter—hence, the name *atom*, from a Greek word that means "not divisible." However, as they probed more deeply, scientists realized that atoms were themselves made up of distinct and minute particles. The desire to learn about these particles and understand the nature of matter and energy led to discoveries that would unlock the secrets of atomic energy.

Albert Einstein.

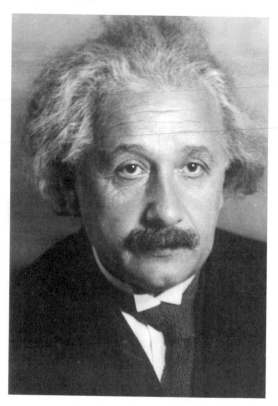

EXCITING DISCOVERIES

Knowledge of nuclear physics expanded during the late 1800s and early 1900s as scientists tried to explain atomic structure and function. Fundamental to their research was the relationship between energy and matter. In 1905 a German-born physicist named Albert Einstein introduced his theory of special relativity, which suggested that mass and energy were equivalent and that a certain quantity of energy equaled a certain mass. He expressed these ideas in an equation that has become universally famous: $E=mc^2$. In the equation, E stands for energy, m stands for mass, and c stands for the velocity (speed) of light, which has been measured at 286,000 miles per second. The relationship expressed in Einstein's equation meant that a small amount of

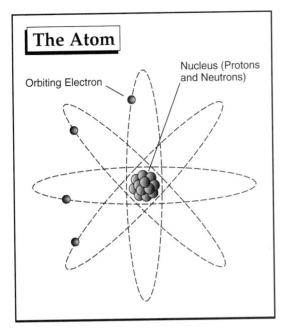

The Atom

Orbiting Electron

Nucleus (Protons and Neutrons)

The three components of the atom are protons, neutrons, and electrons.

mass could be equivalent to a massive quantity of energy. Although people found these theories intriguing, it was not until scientists had identified the components of the atoms that the practical implications of Einstein's theories became clear.

By 1930 two of these components, the proton and the electron, had been identified. Then, in 1932, an English scientist named James Chadwick discovered the third major building block of most atoms, the neutron. Chadwick's discovery revolutionized the field of nuclear research. Scientists found that protons and neutrons form the nucleus, or central mass, of most atoms. Electrons orbit the nucleus in a way that has been compared to planets orbiting the sun.

SPLITTING THE URANIUM ATOM

Other scientists built on studies of atomic structure and radioactivity associated with some atoms. In Italy in 1934 Enrico Fermi began a series of bombardment experiments using neutrons. He reasoned that, because neutrons have no electrical charge, they would not be attracted by negatively charged particles (electrons) around the

Enrico Fermi reasoned that because neutrons would not be attracted to protons or electrons, they would be the key to the splitting of the atom.

atom or repelled by the positive charges coming from the protons in the nucleus.

Fermi devised a neutron "gun," which was a glass tube designed to hold radon gas, obtained from radium, and beryllium. As particles from the radioactive material were emitted, they hit the beryllium nuclei, which then emitted the neutrons.

Fermi and his colleagues proceeded to bombard different elements with neutrons. They started with hydrogen, the lightest element, and moved up the periodic table of elements. Fermi was excited to detect radioactivity when he bombarded fluorine. Elements heavier than fluorine also became radioactive, some more than others. In general, the heavier the element, the less stable it was.

When Fermi bombarded element Number 92, uranium, it proved to be highly radioactive. However, Fermi could not isolate the products created during this process and therefore did not realize he had split the atom.

A Scientific Brain Trust

The people who came together to build the atomic bomb included the most brilliant scientific minds of the twentieth century. Many of them were refugees. Between 1933 and 1944, hundreds of European scientists left Nazi Germany and other Nazi-occupied or Fascist countries. More than one hundred physicists fled to the United States and England from Germany, Austria, Italy, Poland, and Hungary. They included Nobel laureates and other top scientists of the era: Albert Einstein, Enrico Fermi, Leo Szilard, Eugene Wigner, Lise Meitner, Edward Teller, and Emilio Segrè. One of the most famous refugee physicists was Niels Bohr (1885–1962), a native of Copenhagen, Denmark.

These and dozens of other refugees worked with native-born American and British scientists on all phases of the atomic bomb project. The politics of intolerance and repression, which had driven these people from their homelands, gave the Allies a scientific brain trust that was unparalleled in history.

Niels Bohr.

NUCLEAR FISSION

Fermi's work won him the Nobel Prize for physics in 1938. Despite this acclaim, political events drove him from Europe. His wife, Laura, was Jewish, and Jews were being increasingly persecuted in Italy. Moreover, Fermi disapproved of Fascism and did not want to live and work under such a repressive political system. So in 1938, when Fermi traveled with his wife and two children to Stockholm, Sweden, to accept the Nobel Prize, he and his family did not return to Italy; instead, they boarded a ship for New York. Once in the United States, Fermi began teaching and conducting research at New York's Columbia University.

Meanwhile, scientists around the world were excited by Fermi's experiments. In Berlin, Germany, Lise Meitner, Otto Hahn, and Fritz Strassman also bombarded uranium. To their surprise, they found that barium (Number 56 on the periodic table of elements) and krypton (Number 36) were by-products of their experiment. Meitner, who had by this time fled Germany because of the Nazis' persecution of Jews, concluded that nuclear fission had occurred. When uranium atoms were bombarded with neutrons, she reasoned, they split apart and atoms of other elements were formed.

Another matter still puzzled Hahn and Strassman: The new elements added up to less mass than the original uranium. What had happened to that mass? Meitner believed the answer could be found in Einstein's equation: $E=mc^2$. In the process of splitting, parts of the uranium atoms

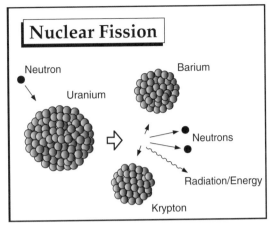

When a uranium atom splits, it breaks up into atoms whose mass is less than that of the original uranium. The remaining mass is converted into enormous energy.

had achieved such high rates of speed that they released energy.

Meitner discussed her theory with Danish physicist Niels Bohr, who, in turn, shared the exciting news with others, including Enrico Fermi, who saw some dramatic implications. Laura Fermi later wrote that her husband commented,

> It takes one neutron to split one atom of uranium. We must first produce and then use up that one neutron. [But what if] an atom of uranium undergoing fission emits two neutrons[?] There would now be two neutrons available without the need of producing them. It is conceivable that they might hit two more atoms of uranium, split them, and make them emit two neutrons each. At the end of this second process of fission, we would have four neutrons.[3]

Bohr and Fermi were among the scientists who wondered if splitting uranium atoms could unleash a chain reaction with tremendous explosive power. Their thoughts turned to what this possibility might mean to the nations that were at war with Nazi Germany. Germany was home to some of the world's foremost scientific research centers, and German scientists were the first to conclude that nuclear fission had taken place. The possibility that Germany might be able to produce a bomb that used the tremendous power of fission horrified these scientists from the Allied nations.

AN URGENT MESSAGE

Another refugee scientist, Hungarian-born Leo Szilard, took decisive action. Szilard had conceived the idea of the neutron chain reaction during the early 1930s, after he fled to England to escape the Nazis, and he had even secured a British patent for the idea of a chain reaction. In 1933 he wrote, "In certain circumstances, it might be possible to set up a nuclear chain reaction, liberate energy on an industrial scale, and construct atomic bombs."[4]

By 1938 Szilard was working in New York City. In his lab at Columbia Univer-

---

"HEADED FOR SORROW"

Leo Szilard, who spearheaded the effort to notify President Roosevelt about German nuclear research, was born in 1898 to a middle-class Jewish family in Budapest, Hungary. Beginning in childhood, Szilard was an eager science student with a keen interest in humanitarian issues.

After moving to London in 1933, Szilard conceived of the idea of the nuclear chain reaction. He filed a patent application, identifying beryllium, thorium, and uranium as the elements most likely to work in a chain reaction. Although his scientific colleagues thought a chain reaction was not feasible, Szilard continued his work after moving to New York in 1938 when war in Europe seemed imminent.

Early on, Szilard realized the dangerous implications of nuclear research. Szilard's recollection of the moment he succeeded in causing a small chain reaction in 1939 appears in William Lanouette's *Genius in the Shadows: A Biography of Leo Szilard, the Man Behind the Bomb*: "We turned on the switches, saw the flashes, watched for ten minutes, then switched everything off and went home. That night I knew the world was headed for sorrow."

sity, he had created a small chain reaction, and he believed that atomic weapons could be built. Szilard was determined to somehow inform President Roosevelt, but he himself was not famous enough to attract the attention of the president. Szilard approached his famous fellow physicist Albert Einstein, who had also moved to America and who had actually met Roosevelt. If Einstein spoke, thought Szilard, President Roosevelt would listen.

On August 2, 1939, Szilard visited Einstein at his summer cottage on Long Island, New York. He and another Hungarian physicist, Eugene Wigner, asked Einstein to inform President Roosevelt that German physicists had split the uranium atom and might be in a position to develop atomic weapons. The three men drafted a letter, which Einstein agreed to sign. Eugene Wigner later said, "Einstein understood it [the danger] in half a minute."[5] Szilard recalled that as they discussed the letter, Einstein remarked, "For the first time in history men will use energy that does not come from the sun."[6]

A final draft of the letter took shape that fall when Szilard visited Einstein again, this time with another Hungarian physicist, Edward Teller. The letter read, in part,

Sir:

Some recent work by E. Fermi and L. Szilard, which has been communicated to me in manuscript, leads me to expect that the element uranium may be turned into a new and important source of energy in the immedi-

Leo Szilard asked Albert Einstein to inform Roosevelt (pictured) that the Germans might be in a position to develop atomic weapons.

ate future. . . . I believe therefore that it is my duty to bring to your attention the following facts and recommendations. . . . It may be possible to set up a nuclear chain reaction in a large mass of uranium, by which vast amounts of power and large quantities of new radium like elements would be generated. Now it appears almost certain that this could be achieved in the immediate future.

UNSTABLE ATOMS

As they studied different elements, scientists found that atoms vary in terms of stability. Some natural elements, such as iron, are quite stable while others are not. As scientists worked with unstable elements, they learned about radioactivity. In 1895 Wilhelm Röntgen, a German physicist, discovered X rays, which are invisible but penetrating radiations. The next year French physicist Antoine-Henri Becquerel found that certain substances, such as uranium salts, emit radiations. Inspired by Becquerel's work, chemist Marie Curie and her husband, Pierre, studied uranium ra-

diations using the ore mineral pitchblende. Radiations from the ore were stronger than those emitted by uranium alone. The Curies concluded that other elements must be present—elements even more radioactive than uranium.

In 1898 the Curies discovered two radioactive elements: radium and polonium. Through painstaking work over the course of four years, they obtained a fraction of one gram of radium. Jointly with Becquerel, the Curies won the Nobel Prize in physics in 1903. After Pierre's death, Marie Curie continued her research on radioactivity and won a second Nobel Prize, in chemistry, in 1911.

Marie Curie.

This new phenomenon would also lead to the construction of bombs, and it is conceivable—though much less certain—that extremely powerful bombs of a new type may thus be constructed. A single bomb of this type, carried by boat and exploded in a port, might very well destroy the whole port together with some of the surrounding territory....

In view of this situation you may think it desirable to have some permanent contact maintained between the Administration and the group of physicists working on chain reactions in America.[7]

The letter went on to recommend certain government actions and urged the president to acquire uranium ore for U.S.

military use. Einstein pointed out that Germany could obtain such ore in Czechoslovakia and the Belgian Congo, which the Germans had seized. The United States itself had only moderate deposits of uranium, but Canada had adequate quantities of the ore.

The scientists took their letter to Alexander Sachs, a friend and adviser to the president, and Sachs delivered it personally. At the time, Roosevelt showed some concern but did not think the government should get involved.

Sachs, by now convinced that this was urgent business, returned to the White House the next day. Over breakfast, Sachs told Roosevelt a story about an American inventor who had approached Emperor Napoléon with an offer to build steamships for his naval fleet. Scoffing at the notion of ships that moved without sails, Napoléon had turned down Robert Fulton's offer. Sachs ended with these words: "Had Napoleon shown more imagination and humility at that time, the history of the nineteenth century would have taken a very different turn."[8]

Silently, Roosevelt wrote a brief note. He handed it to a servant, who left, then returned with a bottle of nineteenth-century French brandy. The president poured two glasses, gave one to his friend, and said, "Alex, what you are after is to see that the Nazis don't blow us up."[9]

A scientist studies a uranium sample. In his letter, Einstein informed Roosevelt that the Germans had access to plentiful supplies of uranium.

The Government Acts

Roosevelt had been moved to action. In a letter to Einstein, the president wrote:

My dear Professor:

I want to thank you for your recent letter and the most interesting and important enclosure. I . . . have convened a Board consisting of the head of the Bureau of Standards and a chosen representative of the Army and Navy to thoroughly investigate the possibilities of your suggestion regarding the element of uranium.[10]

Initially, the president allocated just six thousand dollars for research, and he approved other measures to keep the Germans from acquiring uranium from the Belgian Congo. Roosevelt appointed an advisory committee on uranium, headed by Board of Standards director Lyman Briggs. He also permitted Leo Szilard and his colleagues to meet with a few select military officials, who remained skeptical about the idea of atomic weapons. The claims the scientists made seemed inconceivable: A few pounds of uranium could be made to create an explosion powerful enough to obliterate an entire city.

Chapter

2 "We Have a Chain Reaction"

Slowly, haltingly, work on atomic weapons began, with Allied scientists fearing they lagged two years behind their German counterparts. Before they could proceed, the scientists had to determine whether they could sustain and control a chain reaction. During 1940 Enrico Fermi worked on nuclear fission experiments with a number of other scientists, including Leo Szilard, Walter Zinn, and Herbert Anderson. Through these experiments, they confirmed that the absorption of a neutron by a uranium nucleus caused the nucleus to split into two nearly equal parts, which released several more neutrons and vast amounts of energy. However, the scientists knew that they would need to confirm these tests on a larger scale before they tried building a bomb.

By 1940 the theoretical bases for building an atomic bomb were widely known. Scientists had traditionally shared the results of their work, both verbally and in writing, a custom they had continued into the 1930s. Political considerations now led

Artists work on signs that implore atom scientists to keep their work secret. Scientists had traditionally shared the results of their research with foreign colleagues.

people working on fission (splitting the atom) to conceal their work from researchers in other countries. Scientists in Germany, Britain, France, the Soviet Union, and Japan were all working—separately and in secret—to develop a sustained nuclear chain reaction. The Soviet project, which was led by physicist Igor Kurchatov, began in 1939 but was later stalled when Germany invaded Russia in 1941. In 1940 Japanese physicists informed General Takeo Yasuda, head of the Aviation Technology Research Institute of the Japanese army, that Japan could obtain enough uranium in occupied Burma and Korea to make atomic bombs. The Japanese Imperial Army Air Force authorized research to build atomic weapons in the spring of 1941.

In the meantime, several refugee scientists had become involved in British nuclear research projects, which gained momentum. In 1940 one of these scientists, Otto Frisch, informed the British military that, according to his calculations, an atomic bomb could be made with one kilogram of uranium. He and another refugee scientist, Rudolph Peierls, prepared a report identifying possible ways to design an atomic bomb and produce the kind of uranium they would need for the weapon.

All of these countries had fine scientists and certain key resources at their disposal,

What Happens When an Atom Is Split?

Uranium is a large atom and is rather easy to split. The uranium atom splits into two smaller atoms and also gives off two or three "spare" neutrons (neutrons that are not needed by the smaller elements that are produced, which may include barium and krypton, for example).

A chain reaction occurs as the spare neutrons are forcefully expelled and hit other atoms in their path. The process then begins all over again. The reaction is so rapid that it occurs within one-millionth of a second. This process, called fission, results in the release of energy in the form of heat and gamma radiation. Gamma radiation is the most powerful and deadly form of radioactivity.

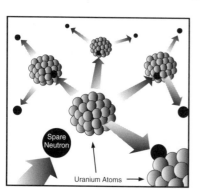

When a uranium atom splits, spare neutrons hit other atoms in their path, which in turn release more neutrons, creating a chain reaction.

Hoping to increase scientific contributions to the military, Vannevar Bush urged President Roosevelt to form the National Defense Research Committee.

but none had the combination of financial means, natural resources, and scientific talent that the United States brought to the effort to build atomic weapons. Moreover, the war was not being fought on American soil, which meant that research could take place far from the battle zones.

Still, by the summer of 1940 Germany was well positioned to develop a bomb. Germany not only controlled large uranium deposits but also had conquered Norway, which had a large factory that produced the "heavy water" that could be used for controlling chain reactions. As German troops crushed nations throughout Europe, the development of an atomic bomb by Allied scientists took on new urgency.

"A MILITARY NECESSITY"

Work on the American bomb-building project accelerated in June 1940. Vannevar

Bush, the head of the Carnegie Institution in Washington, D.C., a scientific philanthropic organization, had urged President Roosevelt to create the National Defense Research Committee (NDRC) to maximize American scientific contributions to the military. Also in June 1940 a larger organization, the Office of Scientific Research and Development (OSRD), was established. Bush, an engineer and mathematician, became the director of the OSRD, whose primary goal was to develop atomic fission.

The NDRC, now a division of the OSRD, was headed by James B. Conant, the dean of Harvard University and a chemist by training. To coordinate the American and British efforts, Conant suggested that they develop a liaison office between the NDRC and the British government. As he explored the question of whether a bomb was feasible, Conant spoke to various colleagues, including Arthur C. Compton, a physicist who worked at the University of Chicago, and George Kistiakowsky, a Russian-born expert on explosives who was at Harvard University. Kistiakowsky doubted that a fission bomb could be built, but after investigating the matter for a few weeks, he told Conant, "It can be made to work. I am one hundred percent sold."[11]

New developments early in 1941 led more people to believe the bomb could be made. In February, Philip Abelson began using a process called liquid thermal diffusion to enrich uranium, which was an essential step in building a uranium-based bomb. That same month, Glenn Seaborg and Arthur Wahl discovered plutonium, an element that promised to be an excellent fissionable material.

James Conant then told his friend Arthur Compton to form a committee and "look over the evidence as carefully as you can, and get a report on atomic bombs into [Vannevar] Bush's hands as quickly as possible."[12] Compton, who had won the Nobel Prize for physics in 1927 for his work with X rays and electrons, invited a group of interested scientists to meet in Chicago in the fall of 1941 to discuss the possible military uses of atomic energy. Among those who attended was physicist Robert Oppenheimer, who was destined to play a key role in the actual construction of the bomb.

Conant was also eager to recruit Ernest Lawrence, who worked at the University of California at Berkeley. Lawrence had won a Nobel Prize for inventing the cyclotron, a device he was using to separate isotopes (different forms) of uranium. Conant told Lawrence that the government was mobilizing for a concerted effort to build a bomb and asked if he would be

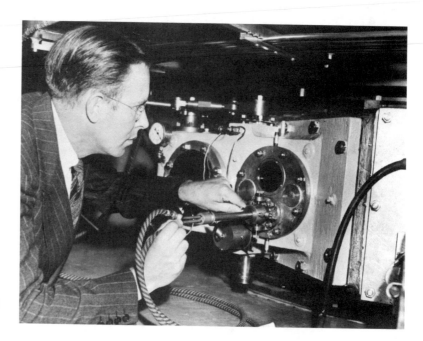

Ernest Lawrence, seen here with his invention, the cyclotron, was asked by James B. Conant, the head of the NDRC, to help with the construction of the atom bomb.

"A Date Which Will Live in Infamy"

Japanese leaders had planned the bombing of Pearl Harbor months earlier. They resented an oil embargo the United States had imposed on Japan as a means of limiting the country's military operations. While Japanese diplomats negotiated with U.S. officials, military leaders made plans to invade Burma, Malaya, the East Indies, and the Philippines—after first disabling the U.S. fleet in the Pacific.

On the day after the attack on the American fleet, President Roosevelt delivered a six-minute-long address in which he called December 7 "a date which will live in infamy." Roosevelt asked Congress for a declaration of war, which it granted.

With the U.S. Pacific Fleet substantially disabled, Japanese troops invaded Guam, Wake Island, and a string of other U.S., British, Australian, and Dutch possessions. The war in the Pacific would see a growing number of bloody battles with tens of thousands of casualties.

Japanese troops celebrate their capture of the Philippines.

willing to devote several years of his life to this pursuit. Lawrence replied, "If you tell me this is my job, I'll do it."[13]

Based partly on the recommendations of the OSRD, on December 6, 1941, President Roosevelt issued a directive to establish the bomb project—in complete secrecy and under the supervision of the U.S. military. The government was now prepared to provide funding and other resources to get this project moving.

On the very next day, December 7, Japanese bombers attacked the U.S. naval base at Pearl Harbor, Hawaii, sinking or seriously damaging eight battleships. Ten other naval vessels were sunk or damaged, and casualties at the base exceeded three thousand. Now America was directly involved in the war.

As the United States prepared to respond militarily to the attack on Pearl Harbor, the scientists who had been gearing up for the bomb project felt an even keener responsibility to help the war effort. Compton later wrote,

We in the United States then saw for the first time that exploration of the possibility of atomic bombs was a military necessity for the safety of the nation. It was then that American scientists began to throw themselves into this exploration with everything they had.[14]

THE S-1 PROJECT

Compton proceeded to organize the "S-1" committee, whose goal was to create a self-sustaining nuclear chain reaction. The first task was to learn how much of a particular isotope of uranium, U-235, would be needed to achieve a chain reaction. Compton asked Samuel Allison, a physics professor at the University of Chicago, to tell him who could provide the most reliable calculations on how much U-235 would be needed to set up a chain reaction. Allison had replied, "No one can answer that question as well as Enrico Fermi."[15]

Based on Allison's recommendation, Enrico Fermi was asked to direct the S-1 project. Fermi was an obvious choice. He was highly skilled in both theoretical and experimental physics, a rare combination. Fermi was also energetic, calm under pressure, and could communicate his ideas well. Compton later recalled that when he visited Columbia University to invite Fermi to join the project, Fermi stepped "to the blackboard . . . worked out . . . simply and directly, the equation from which could be calculated the critical size of a chain reaction

sphere."[16] Compton had found the right person for the job.

S-1, which was part of a group code-named Metallurgical Laboratory, nicknamed "Met Lab," was based in Chicago. Compton declared that the group must reach their goal by January 2, 1943, which gave them about a year.

COMPLEX PROBLEMS

The S-1 scientists realized from the outset that their biggest hurdle was obtaining enough fissionable uranium to sustain a nuclear chain reaction. The scientists calculated the necessary amount of U-235 at 110

Enrico Fermi, seen here working out the critical size of a chain reaction sphere, was highly skilled in both theoretical and experimental physics.

A Scientific Explorer

Born in Rome in 1901, Enrico Fermi's interest in science was apparent even in early childhood when he named Galileo and Albert Einstein as two of his heroes. At age seventeen Fermi received a scholarship to attend the University of Pisa, renowned for its science program. By 1922 he had earned a doctoral degree in physics with high honors. After studying with Max Born in Germany, Fermi began teaching at the University of Rome, where he did research in both experimental and theoretical physics. While working at the university, he met his future wife, Laura Capon, who was a science student there.

In 1934 Fermi proposed his theory of beta decay, stating that when a neutron is absorbed by a proton, it emits an electron and a particle Fermi called a neutrino. As he continued his work on radioactivity, Fermi noticed that when he passed neutrons through hydrogen, they were slowed and became more likely to be absorbed by the nucleus of the hydrogen atom. Slowed-down neutrons showed a greater ability to produce artificial radiation. Fermi's research on neutron bombardment won him the Nobel Prize in 1938.

pounds (50 kilograms). Overcoming that hurdle would be a considerable accomplishment in itself. Not only is uranium ore scarce, but only a small part of the ore can be made suitable for bombs. First, they had to obtain uranium metal from the ore, and only about 50 tons of uranium metal could be obtained from every 25,000 tons of ore. Once it was separated from the ore, less than 1 percent of the pure uranium was U-235; most was U-238, but this isotope was much less fissionable than U-235. The uranium had to be enriched—that is, undergo a process that isolated the weapons-grade uranium, U-235. The scientists needed to find a way to enrich enough uranium to get the amounts of U-235 that they needed for a bomb. At that time, nobody knew an efficient and reliable way to accomplish that task.

Believing that other weapons-grade materials would be needed, the scientists also discussed the possibility of using plutonium for a bomb. Plutonium does not occur naturally; it is a by-product of the fission of U-238. To obtain plutonium in the form of Pu-239, the isotope needed for a bomb, the researchers would need to develop a special and safe reactor.

As some scientists considered ways to produce plutonium, others were working on mechanical processes to enrich uranium. For example, chemist Harold C. Urey worked on a separation method called gaseous diffusion. At his laboratory, Ernest Lawrence tested another process, which involved using electromagnetic separation. The effort to isolate enough weapons-grade uranium and plutonium would consume enormous amounts of time, money, and other resources before the project was completed.

Another problem was how to control a chain reaction once it had begun. Fermi's team had to figure out what material would be suitable for moderating the neutrons in the chain reaction. These neutrons would be traveling at relatively fast speeds, and the scientists would need some way to control their activity. They eventually decided that graphite would be used to contain the reaction, and movable cadmium rods would be used to control the reaction itself.

Besides the uranium that would create the chain reaction itself, the S-1 team needed large amounts of pure graphite, the material that would surround the uranium and help contain the reaction. In May 1941 additional government funding allowed Fermi's team to purchase more graphite. Forty tons of graphite were ordered for experiments on atomic piles.

After experimenting with thirty different piles, the S-1 group prepared for its final and most important test. The group needed a safe, secret place for its nuclear reactor and chose the squash court located below Stagg Field Stadium on the University of Chicago campus. The S-1 team began constructing this pile in November 1942.

The first atomic pile was built on the squash court below the stands of Stagg Field Stadium at the University of Chicago.

BUILDING THE PILE

During the first half of 1942, Enrico Fermi and his S-1 team continued their efforts to construct an "atomic pile" where a chain reaction could be started. They began by building some small experimental piles. As the nuclear reaction project moved forward, more scientists took part. Chemists, biologists, chemical engineers, metallurgists, and engineers were part of the team. Because of the known risks to the people who worked with radioactive materials, health researchers were recruited as well.

To build the pile, scientists and support staff worked around the clock adding graphite bricks, which were made by skilled mechanics, to their creation. Black graphite dust clung to their hands and clothing as they worked. Albert Wattenberg, a member of the group that worked to build the pile, later said,

> We found out how coal miners feel. . . . One shower would only remove the dust; in the pores of our skin would start oozing (sic). Walking around the room where we cut the graphite was like walking on a dance floor. Graphite is a dry lubricant, you know, and the cement floor covered with graphite dust was slippery.[17]

The group was so cautious, however, that other people on the campus remained unaware of the momentous activities taking place in their midst.

Fermi had calculated the size pile they would need based on tests he had done at Columbia University. As the pile was being built, Leona Woods, the only female scientist in the S-1 group, took careful measurements. The construction of the pile must be exact and the measurements precise if they were to succeed.

Finally, it was finished. The pile stood 26 feet tall and had required 380 tons of purified graphite and 22,000 pellets of uranium, placed amid layers of cadmium sheets and placed on a wooden platform. Forty tons of uranium oxide and 6 tons of uranium metal had gone into the pile, and it cost about $2.7 million. Despite all of the expense and effort, one question remained: Would it work?

Fermi's atomic pile cost $2.7 million to construct and required 380 tons of purified graphite, 40 tons of uranium oxide, and 6 tons of uranium.

"WE SHALL BEGIN OUR EXPERIMENT"

December 2, 1942, was a bitterly cold wintry day in Chicago. Inside the squash court, the S-1 group began gathering at about 8:30 A.M. More than fifty people were present. They included scientists, the carpenter who had built the graphite blocks and cadmium rods, and members of the group's health and protection unit. These spectators stood on a small balcony located about ten feet above the floor of the court. On the east end near the instruments stood Enrico Fermi, Arthur Compton, Walter Zinn, and Herbert Anderson.

One man, physicist George Weil, stood on the floor just beneath the balcony. Weil had been assigned to handle the last of the control rods. Three control rods made of cadmium had been imbedded in the piles of graphite bricks to absorb neutrons and prevent the chain reaction from starting until the scientists were ready.

Instruments had been placed at specific places throughout the pile to record the activity of the neutrons passing through. As a humorous touch, the instruments were called Piglet, Roo, Kanga, and Tigger—names from the children's book *Winnie the Pooh*, which Enrico Fermi had been reading to improve his English. A pen was attached to the instruments so that it would pick up the action of the Geiger counters and make a line that showed these changes on a graph. As the counters clicked faster to indicate increasing radioactivity, the pen would move up on the graph, helping the scientists to understand what was happening in the pile.

Several safety features were in place. An electronically controlled cadmium strip that the S-1 group called "Zip" was set to regulate the rate of the reaction. About one hundred feet from the pile, behind concrete walls, stood a group of men holding remote control instruments that would activate an electrical mechanism to put safety rods in place should the reaction start to get out of control. Another cadmium rod, weighted with lead, was attached to the balcony rail by a rope, available in case Fermi needed to

In this illustration, George Weil starts the chain reaction by pulling out the last control rod while the rest of the scientists look on from the balcony.

shut down the reaction during an emergency. If the neutron detectors showed that the reaction was raging out of control, physicist Norman Hilberry stood ready with an ax to cut the rope. Later, Hilberry said that he was sure he would not have to use the ax: "We all knew the scientific work would be all right."[18] Because the reaction would generate heat, fire was another danger. A group of three men—called the suicide squad—was equipped with buckets of cadmium sulfate and other materials to squelch any fire that might start.

Despite these precautions, the scientists understood the risks. Nobody could be absolutely sure the reaction could be controlled. Everyone knew that if they lost control of the reaction, they could die horribly from radiation poisoning or be killed outright in an explosion. The mood in the squash court was serious, and some participants held their breath as the test began. Enrico Fermi later shared his memories of that day with his wife, who described this scene in her book *Atoms in the Family*:

> [Fermi] said, "Presently we shall begin our experiment. George [Weil] will pull out his rod a little at a time. We shall take measurements and verify that the pile will keep on acting as we have calculated."[19]

Fermi grinned confidently as he gave the first order. Weil climbed into position and began pulling out the thirteen-foot-long control rod. The Geiger counters clicked, and the pen recorded the action. Weil withdrew the rod farther, and the clicking speeded up.

Physicist Bernard Feld later shared his memories of these moments:

> When everything was ready, Fermi had the rods withdrawn one by one and he was sitting there looking at the counter. As the counter started to go out and up, finally when all the rods were withdrawn, we could hear the counter rrrrrRRR! And off the scale.[20]

It was then about noon. Fermi, who had remained calm all morning, announced, "I'm hungry. Let's go to lunch."[21] The rods were put back in place while the group took a break.

The experiment resumed at 2:00 P.M. At 3:20 that afternoon, Fermi told Weil to withdraw the control rods another foot. Steady clicking sounds could be heard as the reaction proceeded, and Fermi watched the instruments and made computations on his slide rule. Weil later recalled,

> I couldn't see the instruments. I had to watch Fermi every second, waiting for orders. His face was motionless. His eyes darted from one dial to another. His expression was so calm it was hard. But suddenly, his whole face broke into a broad smile.[22]

Fermi closed his slide rule and told the group, "We have a chain reaction. . . . The reaction is self-sustaining."[23] The reaction continued for twenty-eight minutes.

In his book *Atomic Quest*, Arthur Compton recalled the dramatic scene he witnessed in the squash court:

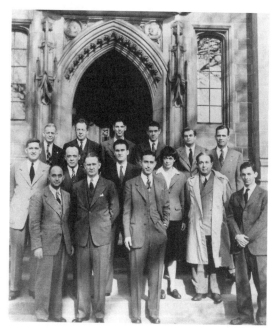

Enrico Fermi (front row, extreme left) and the rest of the Chicago group led the world into the atomic age when they figured out how to induce a chain reaction.

The nuclear pile had behaved according to plan, and they had controlled the reaction. Relieved and excited, the scientists toasted their success with paper cups filled with the red wine Wigner had brought. Most of the people present signed their names on the straw basket surrounding the wine bottle.

Those present understood that their work would change the world. Compton declared that it was the beginning of "a new age," one in which, "the vast reserves of energy held in the nucleus of the atom were at the disposal of man."[25] He later wrote that "the power liberated was less than that needed to light an electrical lamp, but that power marked a new era in man's history."[26]

[The Geiger] counters registering the rays from the pile began to click faster and faster until the sound became a rattle. . . . Finally, after many minutes the meters showed a reading that meant that the radiation reaching the balcony was beginning to be dangerous. "Throw in the safety rods," came Fermi's order. They went in with a clatter. . . . The rattle of the counters died down to an occasional click. I imagine that I can still hear the sigh of relief from the suicide squad. Eugene Wigner produced a bottle of Italian wine and gave it to Fermi. A little cheer went up.[24]

"THE NEW WORLD"

Compton called James Conant with the news, communicated in a special code that they had worked out. Compton said, "You'll be happy to know that the Italian navigator [Fermi] has just landed in the New World." Conant asked him, "Were the natives friendly?" Compton's answer: "Everyone landed safe and happy."[27]

In fact, the "Italian navigator" had managed to develop the world's first controlled nuclear chain reaction ahead of Compton's deadline. However, nobody involved in the project could be sure that they had outpaced the Germans.

3 Desert Laboratory

After the successful test of the atomic pile, members of the Met Lab joined other bomb-related projects. More and more people were recruited as the project

Harold C. Urey, one of many scientists working on bomb-related research, produced heavy water at Columbia University.

steadily expanded. By the end of 1942, scientists were working on bomb-related research at the University of Chicago, Stanford University (California), Cornell University (New York State), the University of Wisconsin, the University of Minnesota, Purdue University (Indiana), and the Carnegie Institution's Department of Terrestrial Magnetism (Washington, D.C.), among other places.

Research was proceeding on several fronts. For example, physicists at the University of California at Berkeley were exploring the properties of plutonium and its potential use in explosives. Harold C. Urey was producing heavy water at Columbia University in New York City. This substance, called "heavy" because its molecules contain a form of hydrogen that weigh more than the most common form of hydrogen, could be used to slow down neutrons in a chain reaction.

The directors of these various projects agreed that they needed to come together and coordinate their work more closely, but where? And, perhaps even more importantly, who would direct the project? The answers to these questions could determine whether the Allies succeeded or failed in their quest for the bomb.

Colonel Leslie Richard Groves (left), an engineer in the Army Corps of Engineers, supervised the Manhattan Project. Robert Oppenheimer (right) was chosen to be the scientific director of the project.

CHOOSING LEADERS

Early in 1942 it became clear that, because this effort would be an industrial-scale weapons-building project, it would be administered by the military. Army colonel James Marshall gave the organization that would work on the bomb the code name Manhattan Engineer District (MED) of the War Department, or simply, the Manhattan Project.

In September 1942 Colonel (later Major General) Leslie Richard Groves, an engineer in the Army Corps of Engineers and an experienced military leader, was appointed as the military director who would oversee the Manhattan Project. Groves had just finished supervising a vast construction project, the Pentagon in Washington, D.C., and he had a reputation for carrying out difficult projects on time and within budget.

One of Groves's major tasks was to appoint a scientific director for the bomb project. By 1942 several influential people, including Arthur Compton, suggested that Robert Oppenheimer be named scientific director. Ernest Lawrence told James Conant that Oppenheimer had key qualities for the position, including "a penetrating insight of the theoretical aspects of the whole program with solid common sense."[28] Oppenheimer, a native of New York City, was one of the most brilliant and versatile physicists of his day.

Groves met with Oppenheimer in October 1942 while Groves was visiting the University of California at Berkeley, where Oppenheimer was a professor and research scientist. Groves had gone to Berkeley to meet with Ernest Lawrence, who demonstrated how his invention, the cyclotron, separated isotopes of uranium. During discussions of how much fissionable material would be needed to make a bomb, Groves asked, "How pure will it [U-235] have to be?"[29] Lawrence replied that this question was still theoretical, but Robert Oppenheimer might be able to come up with an answer.

The two men met in Oppenheimer's office, and Groves was impressed with the

"FATHER OF THE ATOMIC BOMB"

Robert Oppenheimer, whom *Time* magazine would later call the "Father of the Atomic Bomb," was born in New York City, where his father was a wealthy businessman and his mother was an artist. As a child, Oppenheimer loved science but also had wide-ranging interests, including mathematics, philosophy, music, and art. In 1925 he earned his physics degree, with high honors, from Harvard University after completing the requirements in only three years. He was one of a few scientists who were invited to study with Max Born at Göttingen University in Germany, after which he worked with other distinguished physicists throughout Europe.

After earning his Ph.D. in 1927, Oppenheimer returned home and continued to study, focusing on the properties of subatomic particles—electrons, positrons, and cosmic rays. He accepted a position as professor at both the University of California at Berkeley and the California Institute of Technology (Caltech). During the 1930s he published numerous papers and trained hundreds of physicists.

Like his colleagues, Oppenheimer heard about the German experiments with nuclear fission in 1938. His concern deepened as he heard alarming stories about life in Nazi Germany from Jewish relatives who had escaped from Europe. In 1941 fellow physicists told him that the United States and Britain were doing nuclear work; he himself was studying thermonuclear reactions when Leslie Groves chose him as scientific director of the Manhattan Project.

physicist's demeanor and clear scientific explanations. Oppenheimer agreed to head the project. In November, Groves telephoned Oppenheimer to arrange a covert meeting. Locked inside a compartment on a train traveling overnight from Washington, D.C., to New York City, they discussed plans for completing the Manhattan Project, including the need to bring scientists together in one central location.

Although Oppenheimer was officially named scientific director in March 1943, he had already begun working on the project months earlier. The Federal Bureau of Investigation (FBI) and army intelligence had been probing Oppenheimer's background since early 1942 in order to give him a security clearance for this top-secret work.

No scientist in history had ever been asked to handle such a momentous task or to make such challenging decisions so quickly. There was no room for error if the Allied scientists were to achieve their goal.

A Choice Location

One of the first priorities for Oppenheimer and Groves was to find an appropriate location where they could bring together the people working on the bomb project. The site for their scientific laboratory and test areas must meet several special requirements: It must be isolated enough to provide security and have a large proving ground available for tests and cleared land that could easily accommodate new buildings. The climate must be mild so that work could continue year-

Buildings at the Los Alamos Ranch School provided housing for the scientists working on the Manhattan Project.

round. Finally, the site must be far enough from a seacoast so that it would be safe from direct attack should enemy troops attempt an invasion of the American mainland.

Oppenheimer thought he knew just the place. In the fall of 1942, he took Groves to a scenic place in New Mexico near a vacation home he owned. The site Oppenheimer had in mind was on an isolated mesa of the Pajarito Plateau at the foot of the Jemez mountain range. A boarding school for boys, the Los Alamos Ranch School, was located here; the school's buildings would provide immediate housing for scientists working there. The site was about forty miles northwest of Santa Fe, so army personnel would be able to buy supplies there or in nearby Albuquerque. In addition, the U.S. military already owned land at the nearby White Sands Missile Range.

After Groves approved the site, the government paid $415,000 for nine thousand acres of land at Los Alamos. The transaction was completed in December 1942, a year after the bombing of Pearl Harbor and within days after Fermi's S-1 group achieved the nuclear chain reaction. For security reasons, the University of California handled the purchase of the site and acted as the prime contractor so that the university's name, rather than that of the U.S. government, would appear on all of the public documents. The university also hired much of the personnel so that the army would not be involved any more than necessary. Oppenheimer and Groves told the boarding school's owners that the government required them to vacate by mid-February,

explaining only that it was a "military necessity."[30]

Advisers who inspected the site had told Oppenheimer and Groves that the school had enough housing for the thirty scientists originally expected to work on what was being called Project Y. Soon, however, Oppenheimer and Groves increased their estimates to one hundred scientific staff members and about one hundred administrative and technical support staff members, and these numbers grew considerably during the next two years. Clearly, more housing would be needed as well as buildings where the work would proceed.

Army crews worked diligently throughout the winter of 1942–1943 to build housing, meeting rooms, machine shops, laboratories, and storage buildings. They installed electrical and waterlines, plumbing, and sanitary facilities for the thousands of people who would live and work

An army construction worker surveys the grounds of Los Alamos as a bulldozer prepares to grade the site.

A nuclear scientist is seen here at work. Oppenheimer recruited top scientists at elite universities across America.

at Los Alamos. The simple barracks-style houses were painted green to make them less noticeable to outside observers.

As 1943 began, work commenced at Los Alamos with the arrival of the first scientists. Progress was slow at first. There was no fissionable material that could be used to make a bomb, and the plants expected to produce that material had not even been built. To some observers, the task seemed not only formidable but also impossible.

RECRUITING A TEAM

Oppenheimer set out to assemble a group of first-rate scientists and technicians, despite the fact that many talented people were already working on various phases of the project or doing other key war work. He gathered his scientists from the teaching staffs of some of America's top univer-

sities, including the Massachusetts Institute of Technology, Princeton University, Columbia University, the University of Rochester (New York), the University of Minnesota, the University of Wisconsin, the University of Illinois, Purdue University, and the California Institute of Technology (Caltech), among others. Other recruits were Oppenheimer's colleagues and former students from the University of California at Berkeley. The Ballistic Research Laboratory at Aberdeen, Westinghouse Research Laboratories, and the National Bureau of Standards were among the scientific organizations and companies that provided other personnel.

In addition to the American and foreign-born refugee researchers, a team of British scientists that had been working on atomic weapons joined the group at Los Alamos, bringing significant data and expertise. During the fall of 1943, President Roosevelt and Prime Minister

Winston Churchill agreed that two dozen British citizens, including famous scientists like James Chadwick, would be assigned to the Manhattan Project. The project had drawn an international roster of scientific giants: Enrico Fermi, Ernest Lawrence, Edward Teller, John von Neumann, Emilio Segrè, Harold Urey, Otto Frisch, and Niels Bohr, among others.

The men and women who came to Los Alamos made many sacrifices and worked long days in an isolated desert setting with few amenities and for low pay. They had to endure extensive personal security investigations and promise not to discuss their work with anybody, even family members. Their comings and goings were closely monitored. Oppenheimer later said, "The notion of disappearing into the desert for an indeterminate period and under quasi-military auspices disturbed a good many scientists and the families of many more."[31] Yet people agreed to come, both for patriotic and scientific reasons. Many of them viewed themselves as soldiers fighting on the "scientific front." The vital nature of their work was clear. As one scientist, Hans Bethe, later said, "We thought the Germans might get it [the atom bomb] before us, so we were in a race."[32]

Oppenheimer divided the research into different departments and carefully chose the people he put in charge of each division. Robert Bacher headed the experimental physics division, Joseph W. Kennedy headed the chemistry and metallurgy division, and William "Deak"

COURAGEOUS FAMILIES

Families who had members working on the Manhattan Project made many sacrifices. Thousands of women ran households alone or uprooted their families to move with their husbands to Los Alamos and other key installations. Wives packed up belongings and headed for the desert, not knowing exactly what their spouses would be doing or when they would return home. Once they arrived in New Mexico, families lived without many of the conveniences that they were used to and endured shortages of water and other everyday necessities. Women often held other jobs in addition to their household responsibilities.

Schools were set up and other activities were planned for the children so that their lives would be as normal as possible. And families grew as the work went on. Robert Oppenheimer and his wife, Kitty, welcomed their daughter Katherine into the world in 1944. She was one of 208 babies born to families working at Los Alamos.

Parsons, a naval captain as well as a scientist, was in charge of ordnance. Hans Bethe, a German-Jewish refugee, agreed to lead the theoretical department. Bethe (whom his colleagues nicknamed "the Battleship") was known for his careful, deliberate methods of calculating. Under Bethe's direction were five other related groups: hydrodynamics of implosion and what in later years would be called the "super" or hydrogen bomb (led by Edward Teller); diffusion theory, IBM calculations, and experiments (led by Robert Serber); experiments, efficiency calculations, and radiation hydrodynamics (led by Victor Weisskopf); diffusion problems (led by Richard Feynman);

The methodical Hans Bethe was in charge of the theoretical department of the Manhattan Project.

and computations (led by D. A. Flanders).

Newcomers disembarked from the train in Santa Fe, where they were greeted by Dorothy McKibben, who managed the Santa Fe liaison office for the project. Her duties included arranging transportation to and from Los Alamos, helping people to ship their belongings, and orienting newcomers to their surroundings. She later wrote,

> They arrived, those souls in transit, breathless, sleepless, haggard and tired. Most . . . were tense with expectancy and curiosity. They had left physics, chemistry, or metallurgical laboratories, had sold their homes or rented them, deceived their friends and launched forth to an unpredictable world.[33]

Cars took them uphill along a twisting, rough dirt road to their final destination, Los Alamos.

TIGHT SECURITY

Groves instituted strict security measures at Los Alamos. Communication was carefully regulated and code names were used whenever possible. The word *physicist* was forbidden; instead, they were called *engineers* and were also given individual nicknames. Well-known scientists were given new names. For example, Enrico Fermi was called Eugene Farmer; Niels Bohr became Nicholas Baker.

Nobody was permitted to utter the word *bomb*; they called it *the gadget* or *the*

Cars are halted at one of the two guard stations at Los Alamos. The site was also patrolled by mounted, armed guards.

beast. Groves insisted that no information be shared unless it was absolutely necessary. Scientists were not even allowed to speak about their work to their wives or children. Censors inspected all incoming and outgoing mail.

Travel was likewise a major concern. Security agents trailed along whenever anyone left the Los Alamos labs, and people had to pass through two guard stations to get in or out of town. Mounted, armed guards patrolled the boundaries of the installation, which was surrounded by a barbed wire fence. Even on the base, no staff member or family member was permitted to travel freely. The staff understood the need for security, however. Physicist Richard Feynman later commented,

There were little annoyances from censorship and so forth and checking in at gates and all kinds of things. But . . . it was understandable that such a thing had to go on. In fact, most of the complaints was that security was rather lax in places. There would be big holes in the outside fence that a man could walk through standing up. I used to enjoy going out through the gate and coming through the fence hole, and going out through the gate again, and in through the fence hole until the poor sergeant at the gate would gradually realize that this guy has come out of the place four times without going in once.[34]

SMALL BEGINNINGS

Work at the Los Alamos laboratories began with a small staff and borrowed equipment: Harvard University sent a cyclotron; the University of Illinois sent a

Women of the Manhattan Project

Although the most visible members of the Manhattan Project were men, women were involved in all phases of the work. As scientists, engineers, mathematicians, mechanics, and technicians, they worked in Chicago, Los Alamos, and other places to design and construct the bomb. Women helped to produce fissionable materials at Hanford and Oak Ridge and worked in factories that produced other raw materials or products used to build the bomb. At Los Alamos, female mathematicians worked on the calculations that were used in building the bomb and planning the Trinity test. They were part of teams that monitored that test. Still others served in clerical, communications, or support positions in these facilities.

Among the physicists was German-born Maria Goeppert Mayer (1906–1972), who had studied with Nobel laureate Max Born in Germany. In 1939 she and her American husband, chemical physicist Joseph Mayer, left for New York and joined the faculty at Columbia University. In addition to taking over Enrico Fermi's classes after he went to Chicago, Goeppert Mayer investigated methods of uranium isotope separation. She also contributed to theories that were later used to build hydrogen bombs. After the war ended, Goeppert Mayer went to the Institute of Nuclear Studies at the University of Chicago, then to the University of California at San Diego. In 1963 she shared the Nobel Prize for physics with Johannes H. D. Jensen for their work on a theory that explained why some nuclei were more stable than others and why some elements had more isotopes.

Women were significant contributors to all phases of the production of the atom bomb.

Cockcroft-Walton accelerator; the University of Wisconsin sent two electrostatic accelerators. With no fissionable material to work with in the early months, the focus was on basic research as the scientists analyzed the physics, chemistry, and metallurgy that related to the bomb. Later, people would devote more time to technology, in terms of engineering the bomb itself.

The scientists pondered the heavy responsibilities and moral implications of their work. They understood, and for the most part accepted, the fact that they were working on a weapon of enormous destructive power. Joseph O. Hirschfelder, a chemist who worked at Los Alamos, recalled,

> Everyone was agreed on the necessity of stopping Hitler and the Japanese from destroying the free world. It was not an academic question, our friends and relatives were being killed and we, ourselves, were desperately afraid.[35]

Moreover, the scientists believed they were in a race with an enemy who would not hesitate to use an atomic bomb. Eugene Wigner later told an interviewer,

> As for my participation in making the bomb, there was no choice. The original discovery that made it possible was made in Germany, and we had believed that the German scientists were ahead of us in the development of a nuclear weapon. I shudder to think what would have happened if Germany had been first to acquire the weapon.[36]

4 The Race Against Time

By 1944 the bomb project was in high gear. Scientists, technicians, and support staff worked long hours in factories, laboratories, and offices. Groves and his military staff showed determination and ingenuity as they obtained supplies and resources needed for the job.

Years later, physicist Victor Weisskopf tried to describe some of the daunting tasks he and his colleagues faced at Los Alamos:

> What happens in a nuclear explosion had to be predicted theoretically in all its aspects for the design of the bomb since there was no time to wait for experiments; no fissionable material was available yet. The details of the fission process had to be understood. The slowing down of neutrons in matter and the theory of explosions and implosions under completely novel conditions had to be investigated. Nuclear physicists had to become experts in fields of physics and technology unknown to them.[37]

Despite the many unknowns that the scientists were dealing with, speed was essential during every phase of the project.

Oppenheimer later said, "The deadline never changed. It was as soon as possible. It depends on when we were ready, when the stuff was ready, and how much stuff we needed."[38]

Groves and Oppenheimer had to work fast in order to complete the Manhattan Project before their deadline.

Dams located along the Tennessee River provided uranium-processing facilities with the prodigious amount of energy that they needed.

MAKING THE "STUFF"

The "stuff" Oppenheimer spoke of was fissionable materials. No bomb could be built until enough U-235 or plutonium was available. As of 1943, neither of these substances had ever been produced in quantities large enough even to see with the naked eye, much less power an atomic bomb.

General Groves had begun working on this problem soon after he was appointed in 1942. That fall, he had ordered the purchase of 1,250 tons of high-grade uranium from the Belgian Congo. He then hastened to find a good location to build and operate a plant to produce fissionable material. He selected a site near Knoxville, Tennessee, for the facilities that would process uranium. Hydroelectric plants along the Tennessee River would provide the enormous amounts of power needed to run the factories. So great was the need for power that electrical consumption at Oak Ridge would exceed New York City's by 20 percent.

More than one thousand people who were living in the vicinity of Oak Ridge were evacuated by orders of the War Department. Construction on Oak Ridge National Laboratory, which began in February, produced an extensive laboratory facility. Thousands of workers erected hundreds of buildings, and, in the town itself, hundreds of new homes were built for employees. Three plants were built in Tennessee to produce U-235. A nuclear reactor designed to process plutonium for experimental uses was also built at Oak Ridge. This type of reactor took nine months to build.

American industry contributed large quantities of materials, machines, and services to this and other operations for the Manhattan Project. For example, the sixty thousand cylindrical "slugs" of uranium needed at the Oak Ridge plant were enclosed in their aluminum casings by the Aluminum Company of America.

Safety at the processing plants was another big concern. Scientists knew that the particles thrown off by the radioactive materials could seriously damage the human body. The plants were built with thick concrete walls meant to contain radiation. Special ventilation systems and monitoring systems were installed, along with sirens that could be triggered to sig-

In order to ensure their safety, workers were required to wear masks, gloves, and shields when processing radioactive materials.

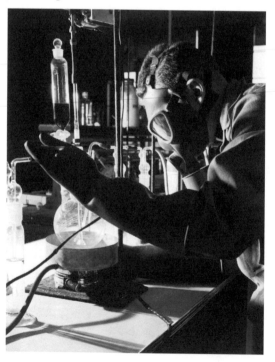

nal danger. Regular checks were done on this safety equipment. Arthur Compton, whose responsibilities included overseeing the plants, worked out safety precautions for workers at Oak Ridge. Workers wore masks, gloves, and shields while processing radioactive materials, and each item of their clothing was specially laundered, decontaminated, and checked for radiation after it was used.

Workers used electromagnetic separation and a process called gaseous diffusion to purify uranium by separating U-235 from the U-238. The process of gaseous diffusion moved along slowly because it required hundreds of steps and thousands of miles of piping. For every two tons of fuel, a small bit, less than one inch in diameter, was produced.

Another plant was set up in Hanford, Washington, where Groves had arranged for the purchase of 780 square miles of land. Located in southeastern Washington State in a remote valley of the upper Columbia River, the Hanford plant was set up to manufacture plutonium using reactors and chemical processing. General Groves, a native of Fort Lewis, Washington, chose Hanford because it was in a sparsely populated location yet had access to enough electrical power from the newly completed Grand Coulee Dam to run this demanding operation.

Many of the fifteen thousand people who worked at Hanford to make and operate the world's first plutonium reactor came from other states. Twenty-three-year-old Don Ebenback was among them. In 1943 he was making TNT at the DuPont pow-

A plant was set up in Hanford, Washington, to manufacture plutonium for the Manhattan Project.

der works in Kankakee, Illinois, when his boss asked him if he wanted to do some top-secret work for the war effort "somewhere out West."[39] Ebenback agreed, even though he did not even know where the operation was located. He later recalled, "We just got on the train, and the only way we knew we were even going to Washington state was that it was on our tickets."[40]

Employees at both plants worked long hours and lived in rough housing and in isolation. Because the work at the plants was so secret, they could not even tell their families what they were doing. The sight of able-bodied men working in a fac-

tory instead of serving in the armed forces caused some men who worked at the plants to be ostracized as draft dodgers.

The first self-sustaining fission reaction (the second in history) was achieved in a reactor at Oak Ridge on November 4, 1943. This large graphite reactor had been built to produce research quantities of plutonium. It would take more than a year before either Oak Ridge or Hanford could process enough fissionable material to make any bombs.

Progress was painfully slow. By March 1944 the Oak Ridge plant had produced a plutonium sample just large enough for the naked eye to see. This rare material was placed in a test tube and sent to Chicago, where it was to be used in some preliminary tests, but it never reached its destination. The scientist who was carrying it had not slept for thirty-six hours, and in his fatigued state, he dropped the tube.

With no time to lose, the Oak Ridge and Hanford plants operated twenty-four hours a day to provide plutonium and U-235 for the bombs that were being designed at Los Alamos. Throughout America, thousands of other scientists, mathematicians, technicians, mechanics,

A NEW AIRCRAFT FOR A NEW WEAPON

As scientists worked at Los Alamos to build a bomb, military officials and leaders of the Manhattan Project considered how an atomic weapon could be transported to an airbase and delivered to a target. They knew that these bombs would be extremely heavy, dangerous cargo.

A new type of aircraft was needed as well, and the B-29, developed in Seattle by the Boeing Company, seemed like the answer. These bombers had pressurized cabins and could fly more than four thousand miles carrying extremely heavy payloads and extra fuel. The new bomber would also need fast-opening doors to drop the bombs.

When the B-29 was first tested early in 1943 in Seattle, the test plane crashed, hitting a packing plant and killing the crew and nineteen workers. Despite this setback, once the B-29 was perfected, two thousand more planes were built. They were used to drop numerous conventional bombs on Japan during the last year of the war. In anticipation for their use in the atomic age, seventeen B-29 Superfortresses were given new suspension mechanisms and fit with a new H-frame hoist, carrier assembly, and release unit so they could carry the atomic bombs.

A Boeing B-29 in flight.

secretaries, and other people contributed time and know-how to the bomb project. Like the people at Los Alamos, they knew that they must work fast and carefully if they were to complete a bomb before the enemy did.

EIGHTEEN-HOUR DAYS

By the end of 1944 about fifteen hundred scientists, engineers, and technicians were living at Los Alamos. Typically, people worked six days a week, often eighteen hours a day. Oppenheimer himself often worked longer hours, pushing himself six days a week with barely four hours of sleep a night. Their days were filled with challenging decisions and projects and, often, frustration.

To ease the strain, workers tried to find time for recreation, including skiing, hiking, horseback riding, and various team sports. They organized parties and enjoyed spontaneous gatherings where they played cards, sang songs, or simply talked about an array of subjects. Practical jokes helped to ease the tension. So did lighthearted gambling, usually bets of a few dollars on whether a particular experiment would work. The scientists also found ways to make the work itself more fun. For example, Hans Bethe and Richard Feynman sometimes had contests to see who could solve an equation first.

People who worked on the project made enormous sacrifices in terms of relocating their families, living in rough housing, and working long hours. Later, many of them said that despite all of the difficulties, they

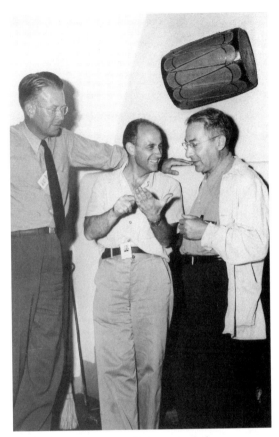

Gathering spontaneously was a way for Manhattan Project workers to alleviate the pressure of their jobs.

valued the experience because of the excitement of discovery, camaraderie, and the conviction that they were doing something critically important.

"OPPIE"

Although Oppenheimer had never been an administrator before, he proved himself quite capable of supporting and encouraging his staff and helping people work together as a team. "Oppie," as he was called, could be seen all over Los Alamos, overseeing the theoretical, technical, and experimental aspects of the project. The tall, lanky physicist continually made himself available to help his colleagues.

At times he might be seen standing in the doorway of a conference room, watching and listening intently. When people were struggling with a difficult formula or theory, Oppenheimer might join the discussion for a while, ask a pertinent question, contribute an idea, or make a few notations on the chalkboard.

Even though much of the time the scientists were working in uncharted territory, officials and scientists who visited Los Alamos were impressed by the speed and efficiency of the teams working on

A FIRST-RATE CREW

Military officials knew that the crews who piloted the special B-29s carrying atomic weapons must be highly trained. A select group of men who had the right qualifications for such a mission were assigned to the 509th Composite Group under the command of Colonel Paul C. Tibbets Jr. The 509th had its own engineer, material, troop squadrons, and military police unit, making it self-sufficient.

During the spring of 1945, the men were moved to Tinian Island in the Pacific by air and sea. There, they practiced for their mission by carrying and dropping "pumpkins"—special ten thousand-pound explosive devices that were painted orange and designed in the same shape as the Fat Man bomb, which resembled a pumpkin with fins. Special fuses that produced an air burst were also installed in these "pumpkins" so that the crews could become accustomed to that feature of the atomic bombs.

One of the crews of the 509th Composite Group.

The design for the uranium bomb (left) was reliable but there were concerns as to whether enough fissionable material could be produced to make it. The plutonium bomb (right) was problematic because it was difficult to detonate.

the bomb. For example, Arthur Compton observed that "ideas originated and developed with startling speed. Equipment that ordinarily requires years for building was here constructed in months."[41]

By late summer 1944, Oppenheimer was often exhausted. His weight had plummeted to 110 pounds on his six-foot two-inch frame. The other scientists and staff at Los Alamos were likewise tired and overworked. Yet none of them resigned or quit as a result of physical or mental exhaustion. Observers claimed that Oppenheimer's skillful leadership was a major reason people stayed with the project. Laura Fermi later wrote,

> Oppie turned out to be a marvelous director, the real soul of the project. In his quiet, unobtrusive way, he kept informed about everything and in touch with everyone. His profound understanding of all phases of research—experimental, theoretical, technical—permitted him to coordinate them into a coherent whole and to accelerate the work.[42]

DESIGNING "THE GADGET"

Day after day, the scientists at Los Alamos wrestled with complex problems. Richard Feynman, who at age twenty-four was one of the youngest scientists at Los Alamos, said there were four basic questions they had to answer before moving forward:

> 1. How big must the bombs be? What is the critical mass for the material needed? 2. What materials would best serve as a tamper [a reflection device to keep all of the neutrons focused on uranium or plutonium]? 3. How pure would the uranium have to be? 4. How much of a shock wave, heat, and light would a nuclear explosion create?[43]

For both the uranium and the plutonium bombs, the scientists had to find a way to suddenly push together enough fissionable material to create a state of "critical mass"—one large enough to sustain a chain reaction and prompt an explosion. They also needed to make sure that the bombs could be set to go off when they were meant to go off and not before.

As they considered one design after another, they concluded that uranium could be detonated by using a simple two-part gunlike device inside the bomb casing. Two subcritical halves could be fired toward each other rapidly to achieve a critical mass. Using a standard explosion trigger, this bomb would be relatively easy to detonate. The design for "Little Boy," as the uranium bomb was called, appeared to be reliable, but there was no guarantee that enough fissionable uranium could be produced to make a bomb, much less more than one.

Plans for the plutonium bomb, known as "Fat Man," were more complicated because plutonium is far more difficult to detonate. The scientists calculated the super critical mass for plutonium at 35.2 pounds (16 kilograms), far more than the plants at Hanford and Oak Ridge could produce. By using a U-238 casing around the plutonium, however, they could reduce the amount of material they needed. The plutonium bomb required a stronger conventional explosive and different triggering mechanism than the uranium bomb, and coming up with a

workable design was taking a long time. "By the summer of '44, there had only been failures in making this work,"[44] recalled Hans Bethe.

Through trial and error, as well as the input of numerous scientists, they finally succeeded. Seth Neddermeyer of Caltech and George Kistiakowsky came up with a promising idea for detonating the plutonium bomb. Fat Man (so-called because of its rounded shape) would contain a ball (core) of plutonium with a neutron initiator in its center, surrounded by a five-foot sphere of high explosives.

As the project moved ahead during the summer of 1944, U.S. military troops fought the Japanese for a group of islands in the Pacific called the Marianas, which included Saipan, Tinian, and Guam. Military officials regarded these islands as the best sites for air bases for planes that could be sent on bombing missions to Japan.

Looking ahead, Oppenheimer predicted that three bombs could be built by the end of the next summer. He told Groves that they would have the materials and other means to complete one uranium bomb and two plutonium bombs. Atomic weapons were about to become reality.

5 Will It Work?

By the end of 1944, some two hundred thousand people were working in nearly forty laboratories and factories across America to finish the bomb. Since its initial funding of a few thousand dollars, the Manhattan Project had now consumed millions of dollars; by the time it was completed, the project would cost $2 billion.

These expenditures and concerted efforts were, however, achieving results. By December 1944, ninety grams of highly enriched uranium were being produced each day at Oak Ridge. Likewise large-scale plutonium production had begun at Hanford. Also in December, scientists at Los Alamos were closer to developing a workable implosion bomb.

In Europe, the Allies had made great strides since the D day invasion six months earlier. Allied troops defeated the German army that occupied France, then

(Left) U.S. infantrymen pose for picture after capturing a Nazi flag. By the end of 1944, the Allies had the upper hand in Europe. (Right) A kamikaze flies through antiaircraft fire as he prepares to crash into a U.S. ship. The outcome of the war in the Pacific was still uncertain at the end of 1944.

went on to liberate Belgium, Holland, and other Nazi-occupied countries. Allied planes bombed German cities continually.

While victory in Europe seemed certain, there was no sign that the Japanese would give up the war in the Pacific. Kamikaze pilots were willing to die in order to kill the enemy, and Japanese battleships also undertook suicide missions. Japan fought resolutely, although naval blockades prevented oil, steel, and other raw materials from reaching Japan and the imperial navy was severely weakened.

The fight against the Japanese promised to be long and bloody. For example, more than twenty-six thousand Americans were killed or wounded in the Battle of Iwo Jima, which raged from February 15 to March 25. In June U.S. forces gained control of the island of Okinawa, where nearly fifty thousand American soldiers lost their lives. U.S. leaders noted that American casualties in the Pacific averaged more than nine hundred per day. Although the scientists working on the Manhattan Project had worried that the Germans would develop the atomic bomb first, it was now increasingly clear that an American bomb would most likely be used against Japan.

A New Commander in Chief

By February 1945 the complete design for the uranium bomb was in place. As for the plutonium bomb, Robert Christy, a member of the theoretical physics division at Los Alamos, had suggested a conservative solid-core design that seemed workable. A talented Polish-born mathematician named Stanislaw Ulam came to Los Alamos from the University of Wisconsin to work on mathematical problems relating to implosion. Ulam suggested that they surround the plutonium core with high explosives that would be cast into spheres (called lenses). These explosives would be wired to fire at the same time. The shock waves from these explosions, coming from all sides at once, would cause the plutonium core to compress until it reached critical mass. The scientists hurried to finalize plans for the detonators, fuses, and high-explosive lenses they would need to build this bomb.

Just as they reached this milestone in designing the plutonium bomb, news came that President Franklin Roosevelt had died at his vacation home in Warm Springs, Georgia, on April 12.

As Vice President Harry S Truman assumed the nation's highest office, he learned about the existence of the atomic bomb for the first time. Secretary of War Henry L. Stimson, who had been briefing the president on the Manhattan Project since 1941, told Truman that an extraordinary new weapon was in the works. On April 25 Leslie Groves met with Truman to fill in more details.

Roosevelt died knowing that the end of World War II in Europe was near. Germany surrendered unconditionally on May 9, but American leaders concluded that the Japanese might fight indefinitely. That conclusion was supported on June 8 during an imperial conference. Japanese government officials pledged that they would "[continue the war] . . . in order to

It was Secretary of war Henry L. Stimson, shown here with President Harry S Truman, who first informed Truman that the atom bomb was being produced.

uphold the national polity, protect the Imperial land, and accomplish the objectives for which we went to war."[45]

President Truman had to plan how to proceed against the Japanese. On June 17 Truman wrote in his diary, "I have to decide Japanese strategy—shall we invade Japan proper or shall we bomb and blockade? That is my hardest decision to date. But I'll make it when I have all the facts."[46] On June 18 Truman met with the joint chiefs of staff, the secretary of war, and the secretary of the navy to discuss military strategy against Japan. They discussed the pros and cons of invading Japan and set possible dates for the invasion. Military leaders warned that there would be tens, perhaps hundreds, of thousands of U.S. military casualties during the initial phase of the invasion as well as many thousands of Japanese civilian and military casualties.

The Manhattan Project, which had begun as a means to defeat Nazi Germany, now offered a way to defeat Japan and end World War II entirely.

Those who advocated using the atom bomb claimed that it would put an early end to the war that had already resulted in an enormous number of U.S. and Japanese casualties.

CAREFUL PREPARATIONS

By the summer of 1945, the bomb was nearing completion. Enough plutonium (about the size of an orange) for one test bomb had been produced at the Hanford plant, and enough U-235 for two bombs had been produced at Oak Ridge. Now scientists were working on casing designs for the two types of bombs. The Little Boy had been shortened from seventeen feet to nine feet, and the scientists felt confident that this bomb would work as expected.

The design of Fat Man had always been more of a challenge. Drop tests were conducted using Fat Man casings armed with regular explosives, but these first tests failed as the bombs went off target. A test of the implosion assembly also sparked concerns that the lens system might not work. However, when Hans Bethe investigated this matter, he reported that the test instrumentation did

not have the capacity to determine whether the system would work.

To see whether Fat Man would work, researchers made plans for a test of the bomb itself. The test, called Trinity, would take place in the desert 210 miles south of Los Alamos in an isolated, secure site called Alamogordo. Predictions on the outcome of the test ranged from total failure to fears the bomb might ignite the earth's atmosphere. Fermi wondered aloud if the bomb might incinerate the state of New Mexico.

In July 1945 Oppenheimer sent Arthur Compton a carefully coded message informing him that they could schedule their "fishing trip"[47] after July 15, depending on the weather. Compton knew what Oppenheimer meant: The bomb would soon be tested.

A crew led by George Kistiakowsky and explosives expert Al van Vessem took high explosives and bomb components to the test site. On Saturday, July 14, two days before the test was scheduled, physicist Norris Bradbury led the group that assembled the plutonium bomb. Preparations took the entire day. Two men carried the bomb's plutonium core on a stretcher to ground zero, the spot where the bomb itself would explode. Cautiously, they assembled the core, making sure they did not accidentally start a chain reaction. They used Geiger counters to keep track of the radiation levels while they were working on the bomb. Bradbury wrote that the process was carried out "slowly" and that he half-jokingly asked the staff to take some time at the site to "look for rabbit's feet and four-leafed clovers"[48] that would bring them good luck, according to old superstitions.

After the core was assembled, a crane lifted it above the center of the bomb, but the core was too big to fit inside. What had happened? Scientist Robert Bacher concluded that the live plutonium inside the core had caused it to expand during the trip from Los Alamos on that hot summer day. After the metal cooled, the pieces fit together.

The completed Fat Man weighed about five tons. Pulleys lifted the twelve-foot-high, five-foot-wide bomb to the top of a one-hundred-foot tower. All night, different staff members took turns watching the bomb.

At the Trinity test site, scientists and workers prepare to raise the plutonium bomb to the top of its one-hundred-foot tower. The completed bomb weighed five tons.

Final Hours

On Sunday Oppenheimer went to ground zero for one last inspection. As night fell, spectators began gathering near the test site. They included people from Los Alamos, military troops, government officials, and one journalist, William L. Laurence from the *New York Times*. The spectators camped in tents and sleeping bags on a hill called Compagna, where they ate dinner. To protect themselves from the intense radiation that would be released during the test, they received suntan lotion and special dark glasses. Strict safety instructions included warnings to lie face down in trenches or shelters during the explosion.

That night, a storm swept through the area, bringing rain and heavy winds. Up in the tower, the bomb swayed. Lightning struck nearby. Physicist Joseph McKibben had spent the night at ground zero guarding the site. At 2:00 A.M., while he was resting, McKibben was awakened by a downpour of rain and the sound of thunder. Lightning flashed in the sky.

After meeting with weather forecasters, Oppenheimer and Groves decided to postpone the test, scheduled for 4:00 A.M. the next morning, by about one and a half hours. They worried about the impact that heavy rain and strong winds might have on the test, their ability to measure the effects of the blast, and the fallout that would occur.

The rain subsided, and preparations were made to go ahead with the test at the new scheduled time. Groves recalled,

As we approached the final minute, the quiet grew more intense. I was on the ground (at Base Camp) between [Vannevar] Bush and [James] Conant. As I lay there in the final seconds, I thought only what I would do if the countdown got to zero and nothing happened.[49]

Countdown to History

The radio frequency that the people at the test site and those back at Los Alamos were using to communicate with each other was also used by the radio program known as Voice of America, which was based nearby. Music by Tchaikovsky could be heard coming from a radio broadcast that Monday morning.

Tensions soared as the countdown began a few seconds before 5:30 A.M. A bright green flare was sent up as a warning signal. Observers saw Robert Oppenheimer put on his protective goggles and stand next to a post, as if to steady himself. He planned to watch the test from inside a trench. Most people were silent.

McKibben was the last person to leave the tower that held the bomb. He made the final connections and threw the switch that started the automatic timer. Then McKibben hurried to his car and drove to a bunker located about two miles away.

A Gigantic Mushroom

At 5:29:45, the bomb exploded, vaporizing the tower where it had been mounted and creating a tremendous flash of white light in the still-dark sky. After the blast, McKibben pulled another switch, which by remote control would activate the instruments designed to measure the blast, then hurried outside to look at the results of the blast. He later recalled, "It was a big ball of fire, brilliantly colored and highly turbulent. The color was somewhere between red and purple."[50] During that moment, McKibben also had the thought that, with this success, the war would end soon.

The atomic fireball soared upward at 360 feet per second. With an explosive force of twenty-one thousand tons of TNT, the Fat Man stunned even those who had built it. Hans Bethe and Edward Teller were watching from the hill station, a distance of twenty miles. Teller wore double-thick sunglasses. He later recalled, "I took off the glasses and looked out. It was like lifting the curtain in a fully darkened room—light streaming in. Then I was impressed."[51]

Observers were amazed and fascinated by the intensity of the light and the vivid colors, which they described as including gold, purple, gray, lavender, blue, orange, and red. They felt a sensation of heat as they watched the expanding ball of fire rise in the sky.

General Thomas Farrell of the army air force observed,

> Thirty seconds after the explosion came first the air blast, pressing hard against the people and things; to be followed almost immediately by the strong, sustained, awesome roar which warned of doomsday and made us feel we puny things were blasphemous to dare tamper with the forces heretofore reserved for the almighty.[52]

For some observers, the results nearly defied description. Farrell called the effects

The bomb in the Trinity test explodes in a tremendous flash of white light. Fat Man had the explosive force of twenty-one thousand tons of TNT.

Seen here from a B-29 flying at about forty-thousand feet, the mushroom cloud rises from the Trinity site.

unprecedented, magnificent, beautiful, stupendous, and terrifying. No man-made phenomenon of such tremendous power had ever occurred before. The lighting effects beggared description. The whole country was lighted with the intensity many times that of the midday sun.[53]

The large cloud of radioactive vapor that would become the symbol of the atomic bomb took shape at about thirty thousand feet. At its peak, the cloud rose about twelve thousand feet higher than the highest mountain on earth. Physicist Luis W. Alvarez was part of a group that viewed the explosion from inside a B-29 flying at an altitude of about forty thousand feet and about twenty miles from the

test site. He drew sketches of the cloud of smoke, which he said had "the appearance of a large mushroom."[54]

Enrico Fermi later described the scene that morning:

I was stationed at the Base Camp at Trinity in a position about 10 miles from the site of the explosion. . . . After a few seconds the rising flames lost their brightness and appeared as a huge pillar of smoke with an expanded head like a gigantic mushroom that rose rapidly beyond the clouds probably to a height of the order of 30,000 feet. After reaching its full height, the smoke stayed stationary for a while before the wind started disbursing it.[55]

During the blast, Fermi could be seen dropping small bits of paper on the ground. By measuring the distances these papers had been scattered by the blast, Fermi was able to estimate the power of the explosion. Amazingly, his estimates coincided with the calculations that were made by scientific instruments that had been placed around the tower and test site.

Leslie Groves saw the test from base camp, where he lay in a trench with Bush, Conant, and others. Later, Groves concluded that the test was "successful beyond the most optimistic expectations of

Following the test, Oppenheimer and Groves examine the remains of the one-hundred-foot tower that had held the bomb.

anyone" and that those who watched it felt "profound awe."[56]

Physicist Robert Serber viewed the beginning of the test without eye protection. He later said that he observed a yellow glow "which grew ominous instantly into an overwhelming white flash, so intense that I was completely blinded."[57] When his eyes began to recover, Serber saw "a dark violet column several thousand feet high." This was followed by shining white clouds. He said that the explosion "had the quality of distant thunder, but was louder."[58]

The roaring noises reverberated off the mountains that surrounded Alamogordo. Hot winds carried an acrid, burnt odor for miles around the site. Observers agreed that the sights and sounds that day were unforgettable. Of the noise, Otto Frisch later said, "I can still hear it."[59] Said British physicist Kenneth Bainbridge, "No one who saw it could forget it, a foul and awesome display."[60]

WIDESPREAD EFFECTS

The flash, which was comparable to the brightness of twenty suns, could be seen far beyond the site, even 450 miles away in Amarillo, Texas. The flash was so intense that a blind girl living 120 miles from Alamogordo saw light. People who saw the unusual bright light wondered if the sun had somehow risen twice that morning.

The blast generated four times the heat of the sun's interior and created a pressure of 100 billion atmospheres. It shattered

"I Am Become Death"

Robert Oppenheimer, who watched the test from Compagna Hill, twenty miles northwest of Ground Zero, later said that he felt faint before the test. Later, Oppenheimer described how he felt after the blast had ended. Len Giovanitti and Fred Freed recorded Oppenheimer's reaction in their book The Decision to Drop the Bomb.

"We knew the world would not be the same. A few people laughed, a few people cried. I remembered the line from the Hindu scripture, the Bhagavad Gita: Vishnu is trying to persuade the Prince that he should do his duty and to impress him takes on his multi-armed form and says, 'Now I am become death, destroyer of worlds.' I suppose we all thought that one way or another. There was a great deal of solemn talk that this was the end of the great wars of the century."

Vishnu in his multiarmed form.

windows located 120 miles away from ground zero. A mile away, ground temperatures reached 750 degrees Fahrenheit, and intense heat was felt by people living ten miles away.

Citizens wanted to know what had caused these strange events—the vivid light, noises, heat, and vibrations. The official story was that an ammunition dump had exploded.

The visible results of the bomb test were sobering. The heat of the explosion had transformed the soil at Alamogordo into green fragments of radioactive glass, which the scientists nicknamed trinitite. A crater about half a mile in diameter scarred the desert. All animal life within a one-mile radius had been killed.

Mixed Emotions

As it became clear that the test had succeeded, the spectators experienced a wide range of emotions. Kistiakowsky, an explosives expert, had bet a month's pay versus ten dollars that the bomb would work. He reminded Oppenheimer, "Oppie, you owe me ten dollars."[61]

The awesome implications for the future of humankind began to sink in for many who witnessed the test. Oppenheimer recalled these words from an ancient Hindu text, the Bhagavad Gita: "Now I am become death, the destroyer of worlds."[62] Physicist Edwin McMillan recalled, "I think it was later that I and many others began to think about the consequences, about what could be done with such a powerful device."[63]

Since security was still a prime concern, the people who had watched the test could not discuss it when they stopped to eat dinner in a nearby town. They reached Los Alamos late that evening. Even then, they could only discuss the test with each other. Later, Laura Fermi described that evening:

> They looked dried out, shrunken. They had baked in the roasting heat in the southern desert and they were dead tired. Enrico was so sleepy he went right to bed without a word. On the following morning all he had to say to the family was that for the first time in his life on coming back from Trinity he had felt it was not safe for him to drive. I heard no more about Trinity.[64]

6 Momentous Decisions

As people stood watching the unearthly blast at Alamogordo, Little Boy, the uranium bomb, was already en route to an island in the Pacific. The U.S. cruiser *Indianapolis* left San Francisco Bay with the bomb on board and delivered it to the military base that had been established on Tinian Island, part of the Marianas, on July 26, 1945.

The Interim Committee—a select panel of scientists and government officials appointed by the OSRD to advise the president on the bomb—had already met once with Truman on May 31. Their job was to discuss if, how, where, and when the bomb should be used. Now that a plutonium bomb had been successfully tested, these issues became paramount.

No Surrender

At the time of the Trinity test, President Truman was in the city of Potsdam, Germany, meeting with British prime minister Winston Churchill and Soviet premier Joseph Stalin to discuss a plan for governing Germany and for defeating the Japanese. He was waiting for some word about the results of the Trinity test. Secretary of War Henry Stimson was the first to receive the carefully worded cable sent from the United States:

> Operated on this morning, diagnosis not yet complete but results seem satisfactory and already exceed expectations. Local press release necessary as interest extends great distance. Dr. Groves pleased. He returns tomorrow. I will keep you posted.[65]

After receiving the cable at 7:30 P.M. on July 16, Stimson rushed to the house where the president was staying and waved the cable in the air. Truman read the cable, then scheduled a meeting with top military leaders who were staying in Potsdam and began informing other key people, including Major General Curtis LeMay, who headed the Twenty-first Bomber Command. Not everyone who heard of the successful test favored actually using the bomb, however. The Allied commander for Europe, General Dwight D. Eisenhower, who was in Potsdam at that time, told Stimson that he hoped America would not have to use the bomb, saying, "I dislike seeing the United States

STRUCK BY A TORPEDO

After the USS *Indianapolis* delivered the atomic bomb to Tinian Island, the ship headed for Guam, where it was scheduled to join the USS *Idaho* at Leyte Gulf in the Philippines. On the night of July 30, while en route to Leyte Gulf, the *Indianapolis* was struck by Japanese torpedoes. The ship, which had not been equipped with antisubmarine detection devices, sank within minutes.

About 900 of the 1,196 men managed to escape before the ship went down. For four days, they swam in life jackets or floated on the few rafts that had been released from the ship. The men endured thirst, starvation, hot days and cold nights, and shark attacks. Finally, by chance, a bomber pilot spotted them and radioed for help. The crew of a seaplane managed to remove 65 men from the shark-infested water. Some survivors were tied to the wings with parachute cords after the fuselage became overcrowded. The destroyer USS *Cecil Doyle* arrived that night. By this time, only 317 men remained alive.

On a website dedicated to the USS *Indianapolis*, survivor Woody James recalls those harrowing days. "The sharks were around, hundreds of them. You'd hear guys scream, especially late in the afternoon. . . . We were hungry, thirsty, no water, no food, no sleep, getting dehydrated, waterlogged and more of the guys were goin bezerk [sic]." When the rescue ship finally arrived, James could hear voices around him screaming, "We're saved."

The USS Indianapolis.

take the lead in introducing into war something so horrible and destructive as this new weapon."[66]

The success of the bomb test affected the Potsdam Conference. Observers noted that after the evening of July 16, President

Winston Churchill (left), President Truman (center), and Joseph Stalin (right) at the Potsdam Conference. The success at Trinity gave the president the confidence he needed to hold firmly to his positions at the conference.

Truman exuded great confidence during the remaining meetings and held firmly to his positions during the negotiations. Churchill, who had likewise been informed about the Trinity test, also expressed optimism that this bomb would end the war on the Allies' terms.

Truman decided he should tell his Soviet counterpart, Joseph Stalin, about the bomb without going into specific details. He later wrote about how he first mentioned the bomb to the Soviet leader:

On July 24 I casually mentioned to Stalin that we had a new weapon of unusual destructive force. The Russian Premier showed no special interest. All he said was he was glad to hear it and hoped we would make "good use of it against the Japanese."[67]

The conference ended with the Allies issuing a final communiqué. As part of the Potsdam Declaration, the Allied leaders offered Japan one last chance to surrender and give up all of the territory it had claimed since 1914. They further demanded that Japan completely disarm members of its military forces, who would then be allowed to return home, and that Allied forces should be allowed to occupy Japan to ensure that disarmament took place at home as well. The Allied leaders made it clear that most Japanese would be treated leniently, stating, "We do not intend that the Japanese will be enslaved as a race or destroyed as a nation, but stern justice shall be meted to all war criminals, including those who visited cruelties on our prisoners."[68] Japan, the declaration made clear, was expected to make reparations to those countries damaged by the military and would be permitted to maintain industries that would sustain the Japanese economy and allow the nation to earn the money needed to pay such reparations.

Japanese leaders met on July 27 to discuss this ultimatum. In response, they declared that they would continue to fight and would not accept an unconditional surrender. Regarding the Potsdam Declaration, the Japanese foreign minister, Shigenori Togo, said, "The government does not find any important value in it, and there is no other recourse but to ignore it entirely and resolutely fight for the successful conclusion of the war."[69]

Japan's military leaders made plans for an all-out defense of the home islands in the event of an Allied invasion. They could deploy ten thousand aircraft, which included some six thousand kamikazes (suicide aircraft). Tunnels and barbed wire fortifications were constructed along the coastlines of the islands of Honshú and Kyúshú. To meet the expected manpower requirements, Japan's draft had been expanded to include boys as young as fifteen and females ages seventeen to forty-five. Troops and civilians were expected to fight on the coast and in the cities, using sticks and other makeshift weapons if necessary. Civilians were shown how to attach explosives to their bodies and fling themselves in front of American tanks. It was clear that invasion would cost both sides a great many casualties.

A HEAVY RESPONSIBILITY

The Interim Committee met to discuss the potential use of the atomic bomb and make its recommendations to the president. Chaired by Secretary of War Stimson, the committee included representatives from the military—Major General Groves and General George Marshall—and scientists—Vannevar Bush, Karl T. Compton, and James Conant. They were assisted by

Kamikaze pilots attend a ceremony before they begin their final flight. Japan ignored the Potsdam ultimatum and prepared for an all-out defense of its home islands.

four other scientists who played key roles in making the bomb itself: Arthur Compton, Robert Oppenheimer, Enrico Fermi, and Ernest Lawrence.

The panel wrestled with the array of military and ethical problems involved. Its members considered three different choices: to defeat Japan without using the bomb; to demonstrate the force of the bomb by detonating it on an island in the Pacific, then giving Japan a chance to surrender (or, alternatively, to use the bomb on an unpopulated area of Japan); or to use the bomb without warning, based on the belief that Japan would not surrender unless it realized the Allies had an unbeatable advantage.

The panel discussed the problems that might arise if they invited the Japanese to witness a demonstration of the bomb

As a member of the Interim Committee, General George Marshall, among others, had to ponder the ramifications of dropping an atom bomb on Japan.

Tokyo after a raid by aircraft armed with conventional bombs. Some members of the Interim Committee thought that an atom bomb would not cause any more civilian casualties than ongoing conventional B-29 attacks would.

over the Pacific Ocean or used it on an unpopulated area. For instance, if Japan knew such a test would take place, it might try to shoot down the bomber or even place Allied prisoners of war in the target area. Also, what would happen if the tests failed? Fermi, Oppenheimer, Compton, and Lawrence joined other committee members who concluded that using the bomb in this way would not be effective.

Using the bomb after giving the Japanese a warning was another alternative. Among those who objected to a bombing without warning was Undersecretary of the Navy Ralph A. Bard. Earlier that year, Bard had written a memorandum to the president stating that using the bomb without warning Japan would weaken America's standing as a nation governed by humanitarian ideas.

One of the most compelling arguments in favor of using the bomb was the belief that Japan might never surrender and that Allied troops would have to physically invade the country. U.S. government officials said that a land invasion of Japan would require about 750,000 Allied troops and promised to be long and bloody. Some officials estimated that millions of Allied and Japanese troops and Japanese civilians might die.

In response to concerns about the number of civilian casualties that an atomic bomb would be certain to cause, some committee members pointed out that damage and loss of life from the atomic bomb would be no worse than the damage caused by B-29s carrying out numerous air raids each day in Japan. They noted that an atomic bomb would not kill as many people as the B-29s that had attacked Tokyo on March 9 and 10 of that year.

In the end, the Interim Committee recommended that President Truman use the bomb as soon as possible and with no specific prior warning. In its report, the committee, with support from Oppenheimer, Fermi, Compton, and Lawrence, stated, "We can propose no technological demonstration likely to bring an end to the war; we see no acceptable alternative to direct military use."[70]

Oppenheimer later recalled that the deliberations were not extensive, although he had some misgivings:

> The actual military plans at the time . . . were clearly much more terrible in every way and for everyone concerned than the use of the bomb. Nevertheless, my own feeling is that if the bombs were to be used there could have been more effective warning and much less wanton killing.[71]

Like many others, Arthur Compton believed the bomb would shorten the war and ultimately save lives. He hoped that after this war ended, there would never be another. Compton wrote,

> I knew all too well the destruction and human agony the bombs would cause. I knew the danger they held in the hands of some future tyrant. . . . But I wanted the war to end. I wanted life to become normal again. I saw a chance for an enduring peace that would be demanded by the very destructiveness of these weapons.[72]

HEATED DEBATES

Other scientists who had helped to build the bomb were also debating whether it should be used. At Los Alamos, people discussed the matter daily. Physicist Luis W. Alvarez was among those who thought the bomb should be used against Japan. He later said, "We had the means to end the war quickly, with a great savings of human life. I believed it was the sensible thing to do, and I still do."[73]

Among those who disagreed adamantly was Leo Szilard, whose concerns had helped set the bomb project in motion years earlier. Before the July test at Alamogordo, a group of scientists organized by Szilard and physicist James Franck formed the Committee on Social and Political Responsibility. They discussed their moral reservations and expressed their conviction that the bomb should not be used against Japan. These were written into the Franck Report, which was given to Secretary of War Stimson early in 1945, before President Roosevelt's death. Roosevelt did not read the report before he died, and Truman, who did read this report, was not persuaded by its contents.

A poll of the scientists who had worked on the bomb project in Chicago was taken in July after the Trinity test. The scientists voted on five different options with these results: sixty-nine people voted that the United States should give a military demonstration followed by a chance for Japan to surrender; thirty-nine people voted to give a demonstration of the bomb in the United States, followed by a chance for Japan to surrender before the weapon was used there; twenty-three people voted to use the bomb and cause Japan to surrender at once; sixteen people voted that the weapon should be used only for a public demonstration; three people voted that the weapon not be used and remain secret.

"The Buck Stops Here"

The ultimate decision to drop the bomb, surely one of the most weighty decisions a leader could face, rested with President Truman. In making that decision, he considered the expert opinions offered by his committee and top advisers as well as other people he trusted.

British prime minister Winston Churchill, consulted at the Potsdam Conference, had also urged Truman to go forward. Churchill said, "The decision whether or not to use the bomb to compel the surrender of Japan was never even an issue. There was unanimous, automatic, unquestioned agreement around our table."[74]

There were also political and strategic considerations to be weighed. With the bomb, Truman had the means to save lives and end the war. In addition, the bomb had cost $2 billion and consumed tremendous amounts of time and energy. The public was still enraged about the bombing of Pearl Harbor, the mistreatment of Allied prisoners of war, and

Because of the public outrage over Japanese atrocities during the war, such as their bombing of Shanghai (pictured), Truman believed that a majority of Americans would approve of his decision to use the bomb.

Japanese atrocities against civilians in Manchuria, the East Indies, and other places. Truman believed that the majority of Americans would approve the use of the atomic bomb against the Japanese. In addition, Truman and Churchill, along with other Western leaders, mistrusted Stalin and worried that he might invade Manchuria and vulnerable countries near the Soviet Union after the war. These leaders hoped that the threat of nuclear weapons would convince the Soviet Union to refrain from such aggression, and improve what Oppenheimer called "the strength and the stability of the post-war world."[75]

Still, people who opposed using the bomb continued to plead their case. Among these opponents was General Dwight D. Eisenhower, who believed Japan was already "thoroughly beaten." He later said, "I voiced to him [President Truman] my grave misgivings."[76] William D. Leahy, chief of staff to both Roosevelt and Truman, also told the president that he believed it would be a mistake to use nuclear weapons, saying, "I was not taught to make war in that fashion."[77] General Douglas MacArthur, the supreme Allied commander in the Pacific, also said that such weapons should not be used against noncombatants.

Truman, who kept a plaque on his desk that read "The Buck Stops Here," made his decision on July 25. He ordered that the atomic bomb be dropped on Japan. The official bombing order was issued to army general Carl Spaatz, commander of the strategic air force. That day, the president wrote in his diary,

President Truman recognized that the decision to drop the atom bomb was his to make.

We have discovered the most terrible bomb in the history of the world. . . . This weapon is to be used against Japan between now and August 10th. I have told the Secretary Of War, Mr. Stimson, to use it so that military objectives and soldiers and sailors are the target and not women and children. . . . It is certainly a good thing for the world that Hitler's crowd or Stalin's did not discover this atomic bomb. It seems to be the most terrible thing ever discovered, but it can be made the most useful.[78]

In a later entry, Truman wrote, "Let there be no mistake about it. I regarded the bomb as a military weapon and never had any doubt that it should be used."[79]

A Unique Mission

By the end of July 1945, the 509th Composite Group, under the command of Colonel Paul C. Tibbets Jr., had spent thousands of hours training for its unique and deadly mission. Because the mission was so important, Tibbets's crew was deemed too valuable to be risked on conventional bombing missions. Other bombing crews based at Tinian saw that the 509th received special treatment but were not sent into combat. As they flew in and out on their own dangerous missions, they called members of the 509th "glory boys" and made wisecracks and

COMMANDER OF THE 509TH: PAUL W. TIBBETS JR.

Paul Warfield Tibbets Jr. took his first airplane ride at age twelve. His father owned a candy business and young Paul agreed to drop candy bars attached to white parachutes from a plane flying across a racetrack in order to promote the business. Tibbets was born in Illinois in 1915. After graduating from Western Military Academy, he entered college to study medicine, but his love of flying led him to join the army air corps in 1937. In 1942 he became squadron commander of the 340th Bomb Squadron, 97th Bombardment Group, and flew twenty-five combat missions in Europe. He was brought back to the United States in 1943 to help test Boeing's new Superfortress B-29. He completed four hundred hours in the air testing the plane, making him the most experienced B-29 pilot in the world. Tibbets was assigned the momentous task of organizing and training the flight crews for the atomic bombing missions when and if the bombs were built.

During the late 1940s, Tibbets served as a technical adviser to the air task force that tested atomic weapons in the South Pacific. Before he retired from the air force in 1966 as a brigadier general, he also served in the North Atlantic Treaty Organization (NATO) in France and carried out projects at the Pentagon in Washington, D.C. Tibbets continued to fly as a Lear jet pilot and aviation consultant as well as rising to the position of chairman of the board at Executive Jet Aviation, based in Columbus, Ohio.

Colonel Paul W. Tibbets is seen here in front of one of the 509th's B-29s.

unfriendly remarks to the men in Tibbets's group.

The 509th continued to remain on the alert and to keep their bombers ready for action, although Tibbets had not yet told them exactly what their mission was. In mid-July Tibbets heard that his flight and ground crews might be separated and reassigned to other groups on Tinian. Some flight crews were short of men, who had been killed during missions to Japan. Military leaders on the base who did not know about the mission Tibbets's group would soon undertake thought members of the 509th could fill these spots. However, Tibbets managed to keep the 509th intact, and they continued to train and wait. On July 25, the day President Truman authorized the use of the bomb, the 509th received its orders in a top-secret communication from General Spaatz, which was also sent to Major General Groves. The orders read, in part,

> The 509 Composite Group, 20th Air Force will deliver its first special bomb as soon as weather will permit visual bombing after about 3 August 1945 on one of the targets: Hiroshima, Kokura, Niigata, and Nagasaki.[80]

Doomed Cities

Even before the decision had been made to drop the bomb on a Japanese target, discussion turned to which city should be bombed. The Interim Committee discussed possible targets for the bomb in May. At first, the list included Kyoto, but

on June 12, Secretary of War Stimson met with Major General Groves and insisted that Kyoto be deleted. Stimson had visited Kyoto, which at one time had been Japan's imperial capital, and he appreciated its cultural and religious significance to the Japanese people. Japan would never forgive the United States for destroying this revered shrine, warned Stimson. He told Groves, "This is one time that I'm going to be the final deciding authority."[81] The president later backed up Stimson. Another city, Nagasaki, took Kyoto's place on the list. Military planners refrained from bombing the cities on the list with conventional weapons because they wanted to be able to judge the full effects of the atomic bomb.

Now it was decided that the first target for the uranium bomb would be Hiroshima, Japan's seventh largest city with a population of about three hundred thousand people. Hiroshima was located on the Óta River near the Inland Sea in the south of Japan's main island, Honshú. The military pointed out their reasons for targeting Hiroshima. The city was the headquarters of Japan's Eleventh Regiment and held supply and munitions depots, transport facilities, and a quarantine station. Hiroshima offered one other advantage as the primary target: It was also the only one of the four cities that did not contain any Allied prisoner of war (POW) camps.

People in Hiroshima sometimes speculated about why they had not been bombed during the war, although they had heard many sirens and made hundreds of trips to air-raid shelters. It was rumored that an American official had

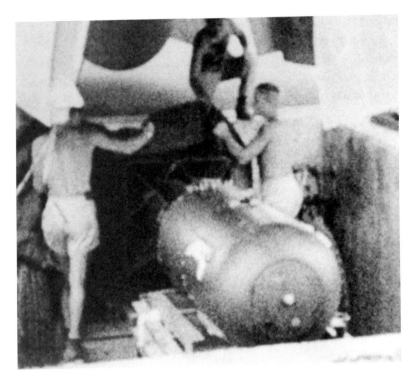

Ground crewmen prepare to load Little Boy aboard the B-29 bomber Enola Gay. *The bomb would be dropped despite opposition by Leo Szilard and others.*

relatives living in Hiroshima and that was why the city had been spared. By August 1945 people were hungry and worn out from the deprivations and difficulties they faced each day. Unusually hot weather added to their distress. Fourteen-year-old Hiroko Nakamoto described the mood in his city in the days before the bombing:

> At night now we seldom slept. . . . At home our air-raid shelter was stifling and full of mosquitoes that bit us mercilessly. . . . I, like almost everyone else in Hiroshima, was tired, very tired, all the time.[82]

As July ended, the Japanese showed no sign of surrendering, despite the portion of the Potsdam Declaration warning that "the alternative for Japan is complete and utter destruction."[83]

Would the bomb be dropped as planned? Some people still fervently opposed it. In Chicago, Leo Szilard, who still hoped to change Truman's mind, appealed to the president once more. He resubmitted the Franck Report, adding a message that said,

> If [a] public announcement gave assurance to the Japanese that they could look forward to a life devoted to peaceful pursuits in their homeland and if Japan still refused to surrender, our nation might then, in certain circumstances, find itself forced to resort to the use of atomic bombs. Such a step, however, ought not to be made at any time without seriously considering the moral responsibilities.[84]

Szilard's pleas, and the efforts of like-minded people, were in vain. On August 4, Colonel Tibbets, leader of the 509th, began briefing the crews and scientists who had been working at Tinian. Tibbets told the group, "Very recently, the weapon we are about to deliver was successfully tested in the States. We have received orders to drop it on the enemy."[85]

After explaining the mission briefly, Tibbets introduced navy captain William "Deak" Parsons, who had helped to build the bomb and was in charge of the group of scientists who had come to Tinian to put it together. Parsons told the assembled group that the bomb "was something new in the history of warfare."[86] It could, he told them, potentially knock out everything within a three-mile area. There were still some important questions. Parsons informed the group that this type of bomb (he did not use the word *atomic*) had never been dropped from a plane before. Nobody was certain exactly what would happen.

Chapter

7 "What Have We Done?"

Hours before dawn on August 6, Colonel Tibbets and his crew walked toward the *Enola Gay* amid bright lights and a crowd of nearly one hundred people, which included military officials, scientists, security agents, and photographers. Tibbets later recalled that Major General Groves had told him there would be a certain amount of publicity, but he thought the scene on the airstrip resembled "full-scale Hollywood premiere treatment."[87] Tibbets's atti-tude was serious and workmanlike. He declined to make any speeches. After a final group photo was taken at 2:20 A.M., Tibbets said, "Okay, let's go to work."[88]

On board the B-29, in addition to the crew, were the Little Boy uranium bomb, which weighed eighty-nine hundred pounds, and seventy-six hundred gallons of fuel to carry the heavy plane thirteen hundred miles and back. The bomb was not armed prior to takeoff; Deak Parsons

The Enola Gay *is seen here after dropping the first atom bomb on Hiroshima on August 6, 1945.*

"Atomic Admiral": Deak Parsons

The man who assembled the Little Boy bomb in midair was a soft-spoken U.S. Navy captain, William S. "Deak" Parsons. Parsons was ordnance chief and associate director of Los Alamos, where his skills as a scientist and engineer helped to turn atomic theory into usable weapons.

Parsons was born in Chicago in 1901, but he grew up in Fort Sumner, New Mexico. His childhood dream was to become a sailor, and he was admitted to the U.S. Naval Academy in Annapolis in 1917. Classmates nicknamed him "Deacon"—shortened to Deak—because of his serious nature and last name. At Annapolis, Parsons met his future wife, Martha Cluverius, an admiral's daughter, from one of America's most famous naval families.

Parsons became a weapons specialist and worked on radar systems and other developing technology. His role in the Manhattan Project was unique: Not only did Parsons help to build the bombs at Los Alamos, but he also accompanied the weapons to Tinian Island, worked with the B-29 crews who would deliver them, and assembled the bomb on the *Enola Gay* as it neared Hiroshima. In *Target Hiroshima: Deak Parsons and the Creation of the Atomic Bomb,* biographers Albert and Al Christman write, "Of all the men on the plane, only Parsons, [Paul] Tibbets, and Maj. Thomas Ferrebee, the bombardier, knew that the bomb was nuclear. Indeed, [Parsons] was one of the few men in the whole Manhattan Project with access to the bomb's entire range of secrets—scientific, military, engineering, assembly and delivery."

After 1945, and until his death in 1953, Parsons, who was promoted to admiral, worked on the first postwar tests of atomic bombs and helped to develop the navy's nuclear weapons policies. According to Parsons's biographers, "[His legacy] lives on in the advanced weaponry and technology of the American armed forces, rigorous standards in nuclear weapons training, and a philosophy of military-scientific cooperation for military research and development."

Captain William S. "Deak" Parsons.

would complete that task once the plane was en route to Japan.

Both the crew and people on the ground expressed relief as the *Enola Gay* took off at 2:45 A.M. Despite its unusually heavy load of sixty-five tons, the plane had cleared the runway and was gaining altitude. Three special reconnaissance planes had taken off an hour earlier to check the weather over the potential targets. Two other B-29s containing special instruments and a plane bearing photographers were among the aircraft that accompanied the *Enola Gay*.

Shortly after 6:30 A.M., the bomb was armed. The radar fuse on the bomb was set to go off at an altitude of two thousand feet above the ground. Now Tibbets soberly informed his crew,

> We are carrying the world's first atomic bomb. When the bomb is dropped, Lieutenant Beser will record our reactions to what we see. This recording is being made for history. Watch your language and don't clutter up the intercom.[89]

Tibbets knew that what he and his crew were about to do would be considered more than an ordinary mission. Unbeknownst to his crew members, Tibbets carried a small box containing twelve capsules of cyanide in his coveralls. He had been told to give a capsule to each of his men so that they could take their own lives in case they were about to be shot down by the Japanese. This would prevent them from being imprisoned and tortured.

"It's Hiroshima"

During the flight, the *Enola Gay* communicated with the weather planes that had gone ahead to check conditions over the three possible target cities. Tibbets received a message that said, "Bomb primary." This meant they were to bomb the first target city on the list. Turning to the crew, Tibbets announced, "It's Hiroshima."[90]

As it approached its destination, the Enola Gay signaled to the other U.S. planes that it was preparing to drop the bomb. In his log, Captain Robert Lewis, the copilot, wrote, "There will be a short intermission while we bomb our target."[91] The men put on the dark-tinted protective goggles that Tibbets had distributed.

By this time, the bomb had been armed for several hours. Knowing they were about to make history, Tibbets and his crew released Little Boy from the bomb bay.

At 8:16:43 A.M. (Japan Standard Time), the world's first uranium bomb exploded into a huge fireball at an altitude of about 1,850 feet above Hiroshima. Within moments, the bombing crew heard intense noises. Violent shock waves tossed their plane upward.

When the B-29 settled down again, the men were awed by the sight outside the windows of their plane. The huge atomic cloud from the blast became a mass of churning colors. Tibbets later wrote, "A bright light filled the plane. We turned back to look at Hiroshima. The city was hidden by that awful cloud . . . boiling up, mushrooming."[92] Members of the crew cried out, "Look at that! Look at that!"[93]

The mushroom cloud rises above what was once Hiroshima.

under the detonation (called the hypocenter) reached seven thousand degrees Fahrenheit, hotter than the surface of the sun. Even a mile from this site, temperatures were hot enough to ignite wood, and people located two miles away suffered severe skin burns. The intense wind from the blast hit the mountains around Hiroshima and bounced back to cause even more damage.

When the bomb fell, sixteen-year-old Akira Onogi was at home with a friend and four other family members about one kilometer from the center of the blast. He later recalled,

> Under the eaves I saw a blue flash of light just like a spark made by a train or some short circuit. Next, a steam like blast came. . . . My friend and I were blown into another room. I was

Some of those aboard the Enola Gay reflected on the implications of this unprecedented event. Lewis wrote, "My God, what have we done?"[94] Another crew member said, "Thank God the war is over and I don't have to get shot anymore. I can go home."[95]

"HELL ON THE EARTH"

The blast, with a force of between fifteen to twenty kilotons, killed an estimated seventy thousand to one hundred thousand people immediately. At least sixtynine thousand people were injured. The heat from the blast was beyond imagining. Temperatures on the ground directly

The intense heat generated by the bomb caused enormous damage in addition to that caused by the blast itself.

"The Ashes of Death"

Besides the deaths, injuries, and visible scars, radiation would cause ongoing problems for atomic bomb survivors (known as *hibakusha,* meaning "explosion affected people") and their families. X rays, gamma rays, and neutrons were released during the explosion. Strontium 90, cesium 137, and other fission by-products were scattered in the atmosphere. The atomic fallout, which became known as "the Ashes of Death," killed and injured people in invisible ways. They suffered from various disorders, including internal bleeding, hair loss, skin lesions, nausea, diarrhea, fatigue, cataracts, and severe anemia.

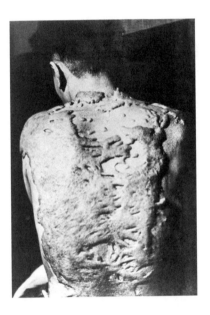

In the years after the bombings, thousands of people died each year or suffered from chronic health problems as a result of radiation poisoning. Exposure to radiation also caused genetic changes that made people sterile or caused birth defects in their children.

The back of this atom bomb survivor is covered with skin lesions caused by fallout.

unconscious for a while, and when I came to, I found myself in the dark.[96]

The house had been blown apart, as had all the homes in the area. Roofing tiles and soil swirled around Onogi. People moaned and cried for help. Digging in the debris, Onogi uncovered his mother, his three sisters, and one sister's child. Outside, he was shocked to see the father of a neighboring family standing there almost naked. He recalled, "His skin was peeling off all over his body and was hanging from fingertips. I talked to him but he was too exhausted to give me a reply. He was looking for his family desperately."[97]

Surrounded by fire, the family fled toward the Óta River. An hour later, large black raindrops fell from the sky. Near the river, Onogi saw people with terrible burns, wounds, and peeling skin. Dead bodies lay in the charred rubble. Survivors used the clothing of the dead as bandages.

Fifteen-year-old Fred Hasegawa, who was heading for a work assignment, was standing on a train platform when the bomb hit. He was knocked to the ground and lost his hearing at that moment. He said, "Everybody's faces were so swollen they didn't look like people. I thought they were dead. You couldn't tell men from women. They were all asking for water."[98]

Taeko Teramae, also age fifteen, was working in the central telephone center that day. She later said,

> I saw something shining in the clear blue sky. . . . As the light grew bigger, the shining things got bigger as well. . . . A flash . . . exploded right in front of my eyes. There was a tremendous noise when all the buildings around me collapsed. I also heard people crying for help and for their mothers. I was caught under something which prevented me from moving freely.[99]

Outside a window, red flames shot up in the darkened sky. A sulfurlike smell filled the air, and Teramae felt the sandy, slimy air in her nose and mouth. Like many others, she headed for the river and tried to swim. Halfway across, she felt faint, but a teacher from the school she had attended came to her aid. Teramae heard agonized cries for help and could not see where she was going.

Kosuke Shishido, a colonel in the Japanese army in 1945, later said,

> I cannot describe what I really saw because it was like hell on the earth. The river was filled with burning logs. It was like a river of fire. People who fell in the river died in the river of fire. We could not help. The bomb generated a strong wind. The wind reflected when it hit the mountains. . . . It was hell. I saw people looking for water and they died soon after they drank it. I saw many people go to the river in search of water and who died. The whole city was destroyed and burning. There was no place to go.[100]

A physician described what he saw that day:

> I saw nothing that wasn't burned to a crisp. [Inside streetcars] were dozens of bodies, blackened beyond recognition . . . dead people who looked as though they had been boiled alive. . . . A man horribly burned crouching be-

This victim of the attack was burned black by the bomb's heat.

side another man who was dead. . . .
In one reservoir there were so many
dead people there wasn't enough
room for them to fall over.[101]

Captain Mitsua Fuchida of the Japanese Imperial Air Force was flying his plane back to Hiroshima after the explosion. He saw a cloud hanging above the stricken city. Looking below, Fuchida was aghast. As he later said, "[Hiroshima] was simply not there anymore. Huge fires rose up in all quarters."[102]

THE SECRET IS REVEALED

The August 6 newspaper headlines told a stunned public that an atomic bomb had been dropped on Japan. Reporters called atomic bombs the "deadliest weapons in history" and declared that a new historical era, "the Atomic Age,"[103] had begun. That day, President Truman issued a press release in which he attempted to describe the bomb and compare it to other, more familiar weapons:

Sixteen hours ago an American airplane dropped one bomb on Hiroshima, an important Japanese military base. That bomb had more power than 20,000 tons of TNT. It had more than two thousand times the blast of the British "Grand Slam" which is the biggest bomb ever yet used in the history of warfare. . . . With this bomb we have now added a new revolutionary increase in destruction to supplement the growing power of our armed forces. . . . It is an

A newspaper from Santa Fe, near Los Alamos, announces the use of atom bombs against Japan.

atomic bomb. It is a harnessing of the basic power of the universe. The force from which the sun draws its power has been loosed against those who brought war to the Far East.[104]

In a special radio address on August 9, the president gave the rationale for using such a terrifying weapon:

[The atomic bomb has been used] against those who attacked us without warning at Pearl Harbor, against those who have starved and beaten and executed American prisoners of war, against those who have abandoned all pretense of obeying international laws of warfare. We have used it in order to shorten the agony of war, in order to save the lives of thousands and thousands of young Americans.[105]

Truman continued with a warning that more destruction was imminent:

The world will note that the first atomic bomb was dropped on Hiroshima, a military base. That was because we wished in this first attack to avoid, insofar as possible, the killing of civilians. But that attack is only a warning of things to come. If Japan does not surrender, bombs will have to be dropped on her war industries and, unfortunately, thousands of civilian lives will be lost. I urge Japanese civilians to leave industrial cities immediately, and save themselves from destruction.[106]

A TOUGH MISSION

Immediately after the Hiroshima bombing, the Japanese did not make any definitive moves to end the war. Neutral nations had been trying to persuade the Japanese government to accept the Potsdam Declaration, and some Japanese diplomats and cabinet members favored surrender and a prompt end to the war. On August 8 Foreign Minister Shigenori Togo told the emperor that he believed Japan must accept the Potsdam terms or the nation would be destroyed. Hirohito agreed, and Togo sent that message to Prime Minister Kantarō Suzuki, who arranged to convene the Supreme War Council on August 9. War Minister Korechika Anami and the chiefs of the Japanese Imperial Army and Navy still refused to accept defeat. They believed the nation might still survive despite the fact that the enemy now had such new and powerful weapons.

It took days before Japanese leaders even realized the extensive damage the bomb had caused. Communications in Hiroshima were totally disrupted and the reports that came back to Tokyo seemed too shocking to be true.

By the time Truman made his radio announcement warning about the threat to other Japanese cities, a B-29 called *Bock's Car* had already dropped another atomic bomb on Japan. That bomb was a copy of the plutonium bomb detonated in the Trinity test. Major Charles Sweeney, the twenty-five-year-old pilot, had flown in an instrument plane that had accompanied the *Enola Gay* to Hiroshima.

Unlike the takeoff of the *Enola Gay*, there were no photographers or high-ranking officials watching the departure of *Bock's Car*. A chaplain prayed as the crew members boarded their B-29. Sweeney was determined to carry out his mission. As he watched the Fat Man bomb being loaded onto the plane, he recalled thinking, "I'd rather face the Japanese than Tibbets in shame if I made a stupid mistake."[107]

Leaving ahead of *Bock's Car* were two weather observation planes that would view the potential targets one hour before the scheduled strike and report on weather conditions. Other planes would accompany the bomber. One B-29 carried

The nose of the B-29 Bock's Car *carried this whimsical representation of the plane's mission.*

photographic equipment and scientific personnel. Captain Fred Bock, who usually flew *Bock's Car*, was assigned to pilot a plane equipped with special electronic measuring instruments. Aboard this B-29, called *The Great Artiste*, was William Laurence, the science reporter for the *New York Times*. A fourth bomber would serve as a backup plane for the other two.

Bock's Car carried an even more complicated and heavier weapon than the *Enola Gay* had dropped on Hiroshima. Fat Man weighed ten thousand pounds, and the crew and people on the ground worried that the B-29 might not be able to fly with its weighty cargo. As the plane lifted off of the dark runway at 3:49 A.M. (Tinian time), it nearly hit the ocean.

There were other perils as well. Unlike the uranium bomb on the *Enola Gay*, this bomb, called "the Gimmick," was already set to explode rather than being armed once the plane was in the air. There was a real possibility that if *Bock's Car* crashed on takeoff, the bomb could explode, destroying not just the plane but Tinian Island itself. Sweeney and his thirteen-man crew, including his assistant, Lieutenant Phillip M. Barnes; copilot Captain Don Charles "Chuck" Albury; a third pilot, Frederick J. Olivi; navigator Captain James "Jimmy" Van Pelt; weaponeer Lieutenant Commander Frederick L. Ashworth; bombardier Captain Kermit Beahan; radioman Staff Sergeant Abe Spitzer; radarman Staff Sergeant Ed Buckley; and radar-countermeasures specialist Lieutenant Jacob Beser (who had also flown on the Hiroshima mission) had seen films of the Trinity test. They knew what this bomb could do. This was no time for mistakes.

The crew also knew that it had to drop the bomb by nonradar, visual sighting of its target, which was supposed to be Kokura. Located on the northeast corner of the island of Kyūshū, Kokura was Japan's principal production source for automatic weapons and held major shipbuilding and naval installations. Sweeney told his men, "Remember, it [the mission] must be executed at all costs. We *will* get the bomb on target, even if we go down with it."[108]

As they headed toward Kokura, the crew faced other problems. Because of poor visibility, only one other plane, *The Great Artiste*, was at the assigned rendezvous point when Sweeney arrived.

Hoping to make contact with the third plane, which carried photographic equipment, Sweeney circled the area for forty-five minutes—instead of the fifteen minutes they had originally agreed on—but the other plane did not arrive. Sweeney gave up and turned toward Kokura.

Suddenly, crew members in the bomb bay saw a red light flashing erratically in the black box containing the switches that armed the bomb. Something was wrong. Alarmed, Barnes and Ashworth opened the cover of the box to find out what had happened. Barnes discovered that two switches had been reversed, and he quickly reconnected them. They had averted a midair disaster.

Next, the crew realized that the city of Kokura was obscured by a dense cloud cover. A member of the crew also thought he spotted Japanese fighter planes in the air around Kokura. To complicate matters, they found that the mechanism for transferring fuel from the B-29's auxiliary tanks did not work. This meant they could not access the extra fuel they needed. Sweeney's crew would have to fly quickly and accurately if they were to complete their mission and make it back to Tinian Island.

Bock's Car now headed toward Nagasaki, which contained major shipbuilding and repair centers. Weather conditions were poor there, too, with clouds covering about 70 percent of the city. By this time, Sweeney knew that he only had enough fuel to make one run over the city before they headed back. They managed to find Nagasaki, and, as Van Pelt checked the radar to make sure they were over the right city, Beahan spotted a small opening in the clouds. He yelled into the intercom, "I've got a hole! I can see it! I can see the target! Bombs away!"[109]

As Fat Man was released on the city below, Sweeney made a sharp turn, just as the crew had been practicing. The crew watched with bated breath as shock waves hit the B-29 and the large mushroom cloud climbed toward them. Sweeney managed to pull away in time. Short of fuel, he headed toward Okinawa instead of Tinian, arriving with a near-empty tank.

NAGASAKI IN RUINS

The bomb missed its precise target by more than one and a half miles but still caused massive damage, mostly in the industrial section of Nagasaki. As was true in Hiroshima, the people of Nagasaki were going about their everyday activities—attending school, cooking, cleaning their homes, working in offices, hospitals, factories, or outdoors—when the bomb hit.

Of the 422,000 people who lived in Nagasaki, 39,000 were instantly killed and over 25,000 were injured. Three important war factories—two armaments facilities and a steelmaking factory—were demolished.

The wooden buildings, many with thatched roofs, caught fire quickly. Hot winds from the blast blew people out of buildings and onto the streets. Flying debris caused more deaths and injuries. People cried out in pain as they hurried to the city shelter for help. That afternoon black

A FAILED BOMB EFFORT

Nearly fifty years would pass before people understood one important reason why Germany did not build atomic bombs during the war. In 1945, shortly after Germany surrendered, fifteen top German scientists, including physicist Werner Heisenberg, were sequestered in an English country house called Farm Hall. The Allies had asked them to write down their wartime research. Heisenberg was among the scientists who told the Allies that he had purposely stalled efforts to build a bomb because he opposed the Nazis.

Unknown to the scientists, British intelligence agents were tape-recording their private conversations with concealed microphones. These tapes were made public in 1992. They showed that, in fact, Heisenberg had been stunned when news reports of the Hiroshima bombing reached the men at Farm Hall. During the war, Heisenberg had overestimated the amount of uranium that a bomb would require. He believed that thirteen thousand kilograms were needed, too much to make the project feasible. When he heard about Hiroshima, he realized his error and did new calculations showing that a bomb was indeed possible.

As historians have read transcripts of the secret Farm Hall tapes, they have reached different conclusions about Heisenberg's real role in the bomb project.

---

smoke and greasy drops of black rain fell from the sky.

The bomb had a power equal to twenty-two thousand tons of TNT, making it more powerful than the uranium bomb that struck Hiroshima. However, there was less damage because there were no mountains around Nagasaki to reflect the force of the blast back onto the city.

This was no consolation to the people who suffered from the effects of the bomb. As was true in Hiroshima, some families lost several members or were even completely wiped out that day. Churchgoers and clergy at the Urakami Cathedral died when the bomb exploded four hundred yards away, as did members of a wedding party and their guests at a building about three hundred yards from ground zero.

Reporter Jinji Sato wrote a story describing the enormous damage to the city and the loss of electricity, waterlines, telephone lines, health care facilities, and other services. Sato wrote,

> At this point, there has been no information released about the nature of the new bomb. Many people have labeled the bomb "pikadon" (flash and bang). Some believe that its power is generated by the sun, since both bombs were dropped in daylight.[110]

WAR'S END

Despite these devastating bombings, some military leaders in Japan wanted to keep fighting. General Anami, the Japanese war minister, addressed the people on August 9, saying,

The remains of Nagasaki. Japan surrendered soon after the second atom bomb was dropped.

> I believe that if we fight through, even if it means eating the grass and sleeping in the fields, we will be able to find a way out. That is the embodiment of the warrior spirit of Nanko, of doing everything to save one's country as long as one has life.[111]

By the time of the Nagasaki bombing, Emperor Hirohito had been advocating a Japanese surrender for several months. Now, the emperor took charge and broke a deadlock in the Japanese cabinet between military leaders and other top officials. Hirohito instructed his ministers to surrender. In an emotional speech to the Japanese Supreme War Council, the emperor said that the "bloodshed and cruelty" of the war must stop and that he would even accept an end to imperial rule to help his people.[112] Hirohito declared, "I cannot bear to see my innocent people suffer any longer. Ending the war is the only way to restore world peace and to relieve the nation from the terrible distress with which it is burdened."[113]

On August 14 the Japanese issued a statement saying that the emperor wished to restore peace and would accept the terms of the Potsdam Declaration. Speaking to the Japanese people over the radio on August 15, Hirohito said,

> The enemy has begun to employ a new and most cruel bomb, the power of which to do damage is, indeed, incalculable. Should we continue to fight, it would not only result in an ultimate collapse and obliteration of the Japanese nation, but also it

On September 2, 1945, the Japanese delegation boarded the American battleship USS Missouri in Tokyo Bay to sign the formal surrender papers.

would lead to total extinction of human civilization.[114]

Formal surrender papers were signed on September 2, 1945. World War II was over at last.

In the stricken cities of Hiroshima and Nagasaki, thousands of survivors were homeless and lacked food and clean drinking water. Bandages, salves for burns, and other medical supplies were scarce, and hospitals and clinics had been destroyed. Many doctors and nurses had been killed and injured, causing a shortage of trained medical personnel to help the many victims.

The number of deaths from the two atomic bombs has been estimated at between 115,000 and 340,000, but an exact count is not possible. Census figures be-

fore the bombings were imprecise; many people moved around during the war. Likewise, some victims were never counted or identified. Besides Japanese civilians and soldiers, Koreans working in the factories and four American prisoners of war who were being held in Hiroshima the week of the bombing also perished.

Atomic bombs had hastened the end of a war that had killed tens of millions of soldiers and civilians. The bombs themselves caused great suffering, and the use of these bombs raised grave questions about the morality of making war with such potent weapons. The development of atomic energy spurred an arms race between former allies that would cause widespread fear and political tensions and absorb huge sums of money and other resources.

Chapter

8 Where Next?

Atomic weapons have not been used in combat since 1945, but people all over the world have been affected by the events that led to the bombing of Hiroshima and Nagasaki. Humankind lives with the disturbing knowledge that atomic weapons can destroy the earth.

The core of a reactor in a nuclear power plant can be seen at the bottom of this photograph.

The power of the atom has been put to other uses. In 1946 Argonne National Laboratory was set up outside of Chicago to study peaceful uses of atomic energy, and many of the scientists who worked to build the bomb went to Argonne and other research centers. Scientists around the world have found ways to use nuclear power as a source of energy, for medical research, and to study the physical universe. By the late 1990s about one-sixth of the world's electricity was being generated by nuclear reactors. Hundreds of commercial reactors were operating throughout the world, and there were 575 nuclear-powered ships and submarines. Studies of nuclear fission helped medical researchers find new treatments for cancer and make other advances in medicine.

CIVILIAN CONTROL

After the war scientists and other Americans, including people who worked on the Manhattan Project in various capacities, asked Congress to shift control of the nation's nuclear energy policy from the military to civilians. As a result, the Atomic Energy Commission (AEC) was

COLD WAR VICTIM

Robert Oppenheimer was one of the scientists who opposed the further development of atomic weapons, including the hydrogen bomb. His political views led to a lengthy investigation of his activities by a congressional committee that questioned people suspected of being either Communists or Communist sympathizers. As a result, Oppenheimer was dismissed from his position on the advisory committee to the Atomic Energy Commission (AEC).

Oppenheimer had been chairman of the AEC since it was founded and had routinely been investigated for security purposes. In 1954, after four weeks of hearings, he was cleared of charges of treason but lost his security clearance. Old reports from the 1930s showed that he had attended some Communist political meetings during the Great Depression years and that some of his friends had joined the Communist Party at one time or another. General Leslie Groves, Enrico Fermi, and the Federation of American Scientists were among his defenders.

After leaving the AEC, Oppenheimer continued his work at the Institute for Advanced Study, where he succeeded Albert Einstein as chairman. As the most extreme anti-Communist hysteria ended, more people agreed that Oppenheimer had been treated unfairly. In 1963 President Lyndon Johnson gave him the prestigious Fermi Award. Johnson praised Oppenheimer's leadership in developing the field of theoretical physics and his unique scientific achievements.

J. Robert Oppenheimer was dismissed from the Atomic Energy Commission because of suspicions about his political views.

established by Congress in 1946 under the terms of the McMahon act (Atomic Energy Act). It set forth provisions for civilian control of atomic energy. In addition to giving technical advice, the AEC influenced policy making. Scientists helped government officials to understand the scientific aspects of various policies they were considering. Robert Oppenheimer was appointed chairman of the General Advisory Committee for the AEC and served in that role for six years. He was one of the scientists who wrote government reports about new developments in atomic energy and explained atomic issues to members of Congress. Oppenheimer advocated using nuclear power only for peaceful purposes and expressed the hope that the very existence of these grim weapons would deter nations from going to war at all. He commented, "The peoples of the world must unite or perish. This war, that has ravaged so much of the earth, has written these words. The atomic bomb has spelled them out for all men to understand."[115]

Numerous other people agreed wholeheartedly, and many hoped the United Nations Atomic Energy Commission, newly formed in 1946, would lead an international effort to ban the production and use of nuclear weapons. In 1957 the United Nations created a specialized agency called the International Atomic Energy Agency (IAEA), which serves as an international forum for scientific and technical cooperation in the nuclear field. Based in Vienna, Austria, the IAEA also carries out international inspections for the application of nuclear safeguards and verification measures covering civilian nuclear programs. The agency was created a few years after U.S. president Dwight D. Eisenhower proposed the creation of an international atomic energy agency in his historic "Atoms for Peace" speech before the United Nations General Assembly. As of 1999, the IAEA included 128 member countries.

Others saw that, with the dawning of the atomic age, peace became the only ac-ceptable path for humankind. In 1947 Secretary of War Henry Stimson wrote,

> War in the twentieth century has grown steadily more barbarous, more destructive, more debased in all its aspects. . . . [The atomic bombs] made it wholly clear that we must never have another war. . . . There is no other choice.[116]

Nonetheless, the race to produce weapons that had already caused so much suffering and destruction was to continue. Far more devastating bombs were already in the making.

THE ARMS RACE

After bombing Hiroshima and Nagasaki, the U.S. military had more nuclear weapons in the works. Three new bombs were produced in September; seven were scheduled for completion by December.

By 1949 the United States possessed two hundred atomic bombs, but another country had "the bomb," too. Aided by spies working on the Manhattan Project, Soviet scientists had made steady progress in developing nuclear weapons. At Potsdam, when Truman told Stalin about the powerful new weapons the United States and its allies had built, Stalin had not seemed surprised. In fact, he already knew about the bomb.

After the war, political tensions festered between the Western Allies and the Soviet Union, which sent troops into several Eastern European countries and installed Soviet-style governments there. These countries, which formed a Communist

ATOMIC SPIES

In 1949 U.S. intelligence agents found evidence that Klaus Fuchs, an Austrian-born physicist who had worked at Los Alamos, had been spying for the Soviets since at least 1944. Fuchs had been part of the bomb-building project in the United Kingdom Atomic Energy Authority, where he worked in the area of weapons development, before coming to the United States with the British scientific team. In February 1950 under questioning, by federal authorities, Fuchs confessed that he had passed secrets to an American agent, Harry Gold. Fuchs was tried and sentenced to prison, where he served nine years. After his release to East Germany, part of the Communist bloc, he became a lecturer in physics.

Harry Gold claimed that he had also obtained information from David Greenglass, who had been a machinist at Los Alamos. Greenglass and his wife, Ruth, confessed to spying after federal agents confronted them with the evidence against them. They, in turn, implicated a young couple named Julius and Ethel Rosenberg, who were relatives of Ruth Greenglass. On March 6, 1951, the Rosenbergs went on trial. Found guilty by a jury, the Rosenbergs were sentenced to death. Both the trial and the sentence sparked controversy around the world. On June 19, 1953, Julius and Ethel Rosenberg were executed in the electric chair in Sing Sing Penitentiary in Ossining, New York.

Ethel and Julius Rosenberg were found guilty of conspiracy to commit espionage in 1951 and were executed two years later.

bloc, were cut off from the West. Travel and trade were restricted and the media were under Soviet control. Winston Churchill referred to this state of isolation as an *Iron Curtain*, a term that came into widespread use.

In 1949, after the Soviet Union tested a plutonium bomb, the competition be-

tween the Soviets and the Americans became more dangerous. President Truman issued a statement in which he emphasized the need to control the spread of atomic weapons:

We have evidence that within recent weeks an atomic explosion occurred in the USSR. Ever since atomic energy was first released by man, the eventual development of this new force by other nations was to be expected. . . . This recent development emphasizes once again, if indeed such emphasis were needed, the necessity for that truly effective enforceable international control of atomic energy which this Government and the large majority of the members of the United Nations support.[117]

A nuclear arms race ensued as these two superpowers—the United States and the USSR—became embroiled in an ongoing competition for international influence. Both the Soviet Union and the United States worked to develop ever more powerful weapons. During the 1950s Edward Teller, who had worked on the Manhattan Project, led the effort in the United States to develop a hydrogen bomb, which relied on nuclear fusion rather than fission. Fusion produced weapons with far more destructive power than fission bombs. The hydrogen bomb was nicknamed "the Super." Both the United States and the Soviet Union went on to build weapons that were hundreds of times more powerful than those used against Japan, along with intercontinental ballistic missiles that could carry them across continents.

Worldwide, the nuclear arsenal continued to grow. Even as new weapons emerged, concerns about radioactive fallout escalated. Scientists were learning

Edward Teller helped develop the hydrogen bomb, or "the Super," which is far more destructive than the atom bombs used in World War II. Seen on the right is the cloud following a test of a hydrogen bomb.

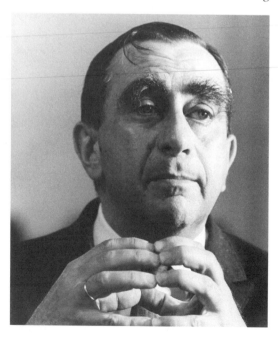

more about the adverse effects of exposure to radiation, especially as bomb victims in Japan developed leukemia and other cancers at rates far higher than normal. Moreover, it became clear that even nations that had no nuclear weapons were not immune to the nuclear threat. Fallout traveled through the atmosphere hundreds of miles beyond isolated nuclear test sites and affected the air, water, and soil. For example, natives of Bikini Atoll in the South Pacific found their homeland contaminated decades after the United States conducted nuclear tests there during the 1950s.

EFFORTS AT WORLD PEACE

People from various countries joined "Ban the Bomb" marches and demonstrations and signed petitions that were submitted to national and international leaders. Having experienced atomic weapons firsthand, the Japanese were frequently at the forefront of these efforts and actively spoke out against the spread of nuclear weapons. Victims of the atom bomb worked to personally promote the cause of peace. In 1949 the Reverend Kyoshi Tanimoto, a survivor of Hiroshima, said,

> The people of Hiroshima . . . have accepted as a compelling responsibility their mission to help in preventing similar destruction anywhere in the world. . . . [They] earnestly desire that out of their experience there may develop some permanent contribution to the cause of world peace.[118]

The children's monument at the Hiroshima Peace Park features statues of two children, one holding a dove, the universal symbol for peace.

Tanimoto urged the Japanese government to establish a world peace center in Hiroshima where programs devoted to peace education and research could be planned and carried out. As a part of this center, named the Hiroshima Peace Cultural Center, the Hiroshima Peace Park was built. The park includes a children's monument built in honor of young victims of the bomb. Japanese children led a fund-raising effort to construct this special memorial after a twelve-year-old girl named Sadako Sasaki died of radiation sickness in 1955. A memorial service for those who died in the bombing is held at the Hiroshima Peace Park each year on August 6. At 8:15 in the morning on this day, all public activities are halted for a moment of silence and remembrance.

Memorials were also built in Nagasaki. A museum in that city contains a collection of photographs and other educational materials relating to the bombing.

SCIENTISTS WORKING FOR PEACE

Although some of the Manhattan Project's scientists worked on new weapons after the war, many of the people who helped to make the first atomic bombs chose nonmilitary pursuits. Some of them expressed horror at the thought that nuclear weapons might be used again and criticized the arms race that developed between the United States and the Soviet Union.

To some scientists, it appeared that their work had not led to a stable peace. After the war ended, Albert Einstein said soberly, "The war is won but the peace is not."[119] Speaking to a group in New York City in December 1945, Einstein expressed these concerns:

> Today, the physicists who participated in forging the most formidable and dangerous weapon of all times are harassed by an equal feeling of responsibility, not to say guilt. . . . We helped in creating this new weapon in order to prevent the enemies of mankind from achieving it ahead of us. . . . We delivered this weapon into the hands of the American and the British people as trustees of the whole of mankind, as fighters for peace and liberty. But so far we fail to see any guarantee of peace. . . . The great

powers, united in fighting, are now divided over the peace settlements. The world was promised freedom from fear, but in fact fear has increased tremendously since the termination of the war.[120]

For the rest of his life, Einstein wrote and made speeches in support of peace and justice throughout the world.

Arthur Compton also worked for the cause of world peace, saying, "It is, to a large extent, the new factors that atomic weapons have introduced that make it now imperative for nations to solve their differences without resorting to fighting."[121] Compton led postwar relief

A patient undergoes radiation therapy. Many scientists of the Manhattan Project hoped that atomic energy would never again be used for war.

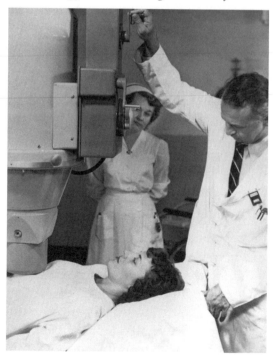

efforts, including projects to help people displaced by the war, and he helped to form an organization called World Brotherhood, whose goal was to achieve justice, understanding, and cooperation among the world's nations. Compton, who accepted a position as chancellor of Washington University in St. Louis in 1945, hoped that nuclear reactors would provide energy and help researchers find ways to diagnose and treat diseases but would never again be used in the manufacture of weapons.

Still others believed that only by working together could nations prevent even more destructive wars than the one that had just ended. Niels Bohr had begun urging that nuclear weapons be controlled even before World War II ended. He had approached both President Roosevelt and Prime Minister Churchill to discuss the need for international cooperation. In 1950 Bohr published an open letter addressed to the United Nations, in which he urged the UN to work for a world free of nuclear weapons. From his office in Copenhagen, Bohr led efforts to find constructive, peaceful uses for nuclear energy. He organized the first Atoms for Peace world conference, held in Geneva, Switzerland, in 1955. In 1957 he received the first U.S. Atoms for Peace Award.

For several months after the war, Enrico Fermi served on a committee that advised President Truman on nuclear policies, including nuclear safety. Fermi then returned to teaching and research. In 1946 he received the U.S. Congressional Medal of Merit, the highest honor given to civilians. During the late 1940s Fermi joined Oppenheimer and other scientists who opposed development of the hydrogen bomb. In 1954 the AEC gave Fermi a special award, recognizing him as the person who contributed the most to the development, use, and control of atomic energy. When he died that same year, the AEC named this the Fermi Award, to be given in his honor each year to someone whose contributions in the field of nuclear energy are deemed worthy of recognition.

Hans Bethe, who returned to teaching physics after the war, reentered the political scene in 1949. He served on a committee that advised President Truman on the hydrogen bomb. Bethe joined those in the majority who advised Truman to postpone building this new bomb, a recommendation the president did not follow. Bethe later changed his mind when he became convinced that the Soviet Union planned to build hydrogen bombs. Bethe continued to lecture on the role of physics in international politics and made speeches supporting treaties to end nuclear proliferation. In 1994, at age eighty-eight, Bethe published an open letter urging that nuclear weapons never be used again. In his letter, he wrote,

> I call on all scientists in all countries to cease and desist from work creating, developing, improving and manufacturing further nuclear weapons; and, for that matter, other weapons of potential mass destruction such as chemical and biological weapons.[122]

After the war, the brilliant Leo Szilard pursued new studies in biology, applying his knowledge of physics to that field. In 1956 he was appointed professor of biophysics at the Enrico Fermi Institute at the University of Chicago. Four years later Szilard received the Atoms for Peace Award. He continued to remain politically active and urged scientists from all disciplines to examine how their discoveries affected humanity. Szilard came up with the idea of the direct Moscow-Washington telephone hot line so that leaders of the superpowers could speak directly to one another in case of a nuclear confrontation or accident. In 1962, two years before his death, Szilard founded the Council for Abolishing War (later renamed the Council for a Livable World).

A PERILOUS WORLD

During the 1950s and 1960s, fear of nuclear war grew into almost a national obsession. Americans speculated about which cities or regions of the country might be targets.

Some people built backyard bomb shelters to house their families in case of nuclear attacks. In 1955 magazine ads offered do-it-yourself bomb shelters ranging from about two thousand to three thousand dollars. Nationwide, about 1 million households owned shelters as of 1960.

American schoolchildren were drilled on what to do in the event of a nuclear attack. A filmstrip called "Survival Under Nuclear Attack" was made available in schools, and students practiced dropping to the ground or floor or hurrying into fallout shelters. "Duck and cover" became

a well-known civil defense slogan. A film by that same name, featuring Bert the Turtle showed young children how to take cover from flying glass and other debris during an attack. A pamphlet featuring cartoon strips with Bert the Turtle was designed for young people and the duck-and-cover theme song was available as sheet music.

Newer and more powerful weapons proliferated, including intercontinental ballistic missiles capable of carrying nuclear warheads across continents. New submarines had the capacity to transport missiles long distances, where they could be launched from the sea. As new offensive weapons were created, scientists worked on defensive systems that might protect people from nuclear attacks.

AN UNENDING DEBATE

The debate over the use of atomic bombs in World War II continues to this day. Supporters of the decision to use the bomb say that the bombings of Hiroshima and Nagasaki were the act of a war-weary and beleaguered government. Truman and his supporters saw the bomb as a necessary evil, a way to quickly end the war and save lives. Many historians have since concluded that any president facing the same decision, with the same information and under the same circumstances, would have done what Truman did. They point out that, had the war continued, with tens of thousands more American casualties, and had people learned that Truman had refused to use a weapon that could have prevented these losses, he would have been despised and probably impeached.

Some critics contend that using atomic weapons was an immoral act under any circumstances. They argue that, by the summer of 1945, Japan was already defeated and would have surrendered fairly soon. These critics also claim that the Japanese were not given enough time to surrender, especially after the Hiroshima bombing. Some critics allege that Truman

An intercontinental ballistic missile is test-fired. Newer and more powerful nuclear weapons were developed in the decades following World War II.

exaggerated the number of casualties that would have occurred in the event of a land invasion.

Defenders of Truman's decision to use the bomb note that there is no evidence that top military advisers told the president that using atomic bombs would be either immoral or militarily unnecessary. Some of these advisers, though, did express concerns about the consequences should the bomb fail to explode. They had worried that the Japanese would be able to analyze the bomb and use that knowledge to build their own atomic weapons.

Supporters of the decision to use the bombs also point out that, during the war, intense use of conventional bombs had also leveled cities and killed thousands of people.

The scientists themselves continued to debate the issues in the years after the bombings. For example, Oppenheimer later reflected, "I believe it was an error that Truman did not ask Stalin to carry on further talks with Japan, and also that the warning to Japan was completely inadequate."[123] Oppenheimer noted that atomic energy held the potential for both good and evil and commented on the dilemmas posed by new discoveries. In 1946, when he received the Presidential Medal of Merit for his work on the Manhattan Project, Oppenheimer told journalists, "I'm a little scared of what we built. . . . A scientist cannot hold back progress because he fears what the world will do with his discoveries."[124]

Other scientists also shared their misgivings. Hans Bethe has said, "It is true. To make weapons of such destructive power is a sin, but somehow we have to live with it."[125]

Some people stress that there is no way to change what happened, and humankind must try to learn from this shattering event and prevent such weapons from being used in the future. Biophysicist Alvin Weinberg, who worked on the Manhattan Project, says,

> In recent years, I've argued that dropping the bomb was the proper thing to do because it was the only way to impress on humanity the terrible nature of nuclear weapons. We have to invest them with the force of religious taboos, which are the only things strong enough to last for millennia. The images of Hiroshima have that force. It's the only way to keep nuclear weapons from ever being used again.[126]

The bombings' survivors have urged people to learn from their tragic experience about the importance of settling differences without violence. One survivor said,

> The bomb dropped on Nagasaki may have served the purpose of writing off all future nuclear wars. We here are somewhat consoled by the fact that we may have sacrificed ourselves for the sake of the entire world.[127]

Toward a Safer World

Even as the superpowers threatened one another with nuclear annihilation, they slowly worked toward reducing tensions. In 1963 the United States and the Soviet Union signed a limited test-ban agreement in which they pledged not to test nuclear weapons in the seas or in space and to limit underground tests. Four years later, they agreed not to send any nuclear weapons into orbit in outer space.

In 1968 both countries, along with France, Great Britain, and 124 other countries, signed the Non-Proliferation Treaty, which was designed to prevent more countries from developing nuclear weapons. In time, other countries joined them.

New treaties were painstakingly discussed and ratified. In 1972 the two superpowers agreed to slow the rate of

The leaders of the United States and the Soviet Union, Richard Nixon and Leonid Brezhnev, are seen here after the signing of the SALT I treaty in 1972.

weapons production. The Strategic Arms Limitations Talks (SALT) set a limit on the number of long-range ground and seaborne missiles each country would amass. SALT I was signed that same year.

Limiting the growth of nuclear weapons was widely applauded, but antinuclear activists had long hoped for an agreement to reduce the number of existing weapons, which, by 1989, had reached fifty thousand. That year brought talks that led to such an agreement, known as the Strategic Arms Reduction Treaty (START), which was signed in 1991.

By the 1990s the economic cost of the arms race was immense. The United States had spent about $350 billion on nuclear weapons. This was about twice as much as the nation spent on space exploration during the same years. About $13.5 trillion had been spent on related military hardware, such as new missile systems and new types of bombers. Four hundred uranium mines had been opened and 60 million tons of uranium ore had been used in weapons. By 1999, with an arsenal of about 10,400 warheads, the nation was spending about $35 billion annually just to maintain the weapons in its arsenal.

When the cold war ended, there were some seventy thousand nuclear warheads throughout the world. Although the danger that the superpowers would wage nuclear war had diminished, significant problems remained and new ones emerged. Stockpiles of weapons needed to be safely dismantled and the radioactive components had to be disposed of. Nations on both sides of the cold war faced the problems of safely disposing of

A Pakistani man protests the testing of a nuclear device by his country near the end of the twentieth century.

nuclear wastes that are the by-products of weapons production and preventing dangerous materials from being stolen or mishandled.

Other nuclear threats still plague humankind. Intelligence agents, for example, have reported that Russian citizens had sold plutonium, and some plutonium has been reported missing from Russian warehouses. The danger that this missing plutonium might be acquired by other nations seeking to develop nuclear weapons is real. Nations such as Iraq, Iran, and North Korea have shown interest in joining the "nuclear club." Officials worry that terrorists might acquire and use nuclear weapons against the United States and others they perceive as their enemies.

Despite nonproliferation efforts, the number of nuclear nations, which includes the United States, Russia, France, Britain, China, India, and Pakistan, continues to grow. In 1998 Pakistan tested its first nuclear device. India responded with a new nuclear test of its own. Other countries, including Israel and South Africa, are thought to possess nuclear weapons, although they have never acknowledged this as a fact. On the other hand, some nations, including Japan, who could easily build their own nuclear weapons have chosen not to do so.

As a new millenium began, people around the world hoped that the nuclear threat would diminish as more weapons were dismantled and international organizations worked to resolve conflicts between peoples without the use of force.

Notes

Introduction: Turbulent Times

1. Quoted in John A. Garraty, *The American Nation: A History of the United States Since 1865.* New York: Harper & Row, 1979, p. 683.

2. Quoted in Garraty, *The American Nation,* p. 684.

Chapter 1: "Energy That Does Not Come from the Sun"

3. Quoted in Laura Capon Fermi, *Atoms in the Family: My Life with Enrico Fermi.* Chicago: University of Chicago Press, 1954, pp. 158–59.

4. Quoted in William Lanouette, *Genius in the Shadows: A Biography of Leo Szilard, the Man Behind the Bomb.* Chicago: University of Chicago Press, 1994, p. 134.

5. Quoted in Oak Ridge National Laboratory, "The Forties: War and Peace." www.ornl.gov/swords/forties.html.

6. Quoted in Fermi, *Atoms in the Family,* p. 166.

7. Albert Einstein, "Letter to President Roosevelt," Public Record, Argonne National Laboratory.

8. Quoted in Dan Kurzman, *Day of the Bomb: Countdown to Hiroshima.* New York: McGraw-Hill, 1986, p. 30.

9. Quoted in James M. Burns, *Roosevelt: The Soldier of Freedom.* New York: Harcourt, Brace, 1970, p. 250.

10. Quoted in ThinkQuest Team 20920, "President Roosevelt's Response to Einstein," *The History and Making of the Atomic Bomb.* http://library.advanced.org/20920/roseveltltr.html.

Chapter 2: "We Have a Chain Reaction"

11. Quoted in James Hershberg, *James B. Co-*nant: Harvard to Hiroshima and Making of the Nuclear Age.* New York: Knopf, 1993, p. 149.

12. Quoted in Arthur Holly Compton, *Atomic Quest.* New York: Oxford University Press, 1956, pp. 8–9.

13. Quoted in Hershberg, *James B. Conant,* p. 150.

14. Compton, *Atomic Quest,* p. 11.

15. Quoted in Compton, *Atomic Quest,* p. 54.

16. Quoted in Argonne National Laboratory, "The 'Last Universal Scientist' Takes Charge," *Frontiers,* 1996. www.anl.gov/OPA/frontiers 96/unisci.html.

17. Quoted in Corbin Allardice and Edward R. Trapnell, "The First Atomic Pile: An Eyewitness Account Revealed by Some of the Participants and Narratively Recorded." Washington, DC: U.S. Atomic Energy Commission, November 1949, p. 3.

18. Quoted in Argonne National Laboratory, "Piglet and the Pumpkin Field," *Frontiers,* 1996. www.anl.gov.80/OPA/frontiers 96/piglet.html.

19. Fermi, *Atoms in the Family,* p. 196.

20. Quoted in Atomic Archive, "Reflections of the Nuclear Age." http://atomicarchive.com//AAReflection.shtml.

21. Quoted in Allardice and Trapnell, "The First Atomic Pile," p. 5.

22. Quoted in Allardice and Trapnell, "The First Atomic Pile," p. 5.

23. Quoted in Allardice and Trapnell, "The First Atomic Pile," p. 6.

24. Compton, *Atomic Quest,* pp. 142–43.

25. Compton, *Atomic Quest,* p. 149.

26. Compton, *Atomic Quest,* p. 143.

27. Compton, *Atomic Quest,* p. 144.

Chapter 3: Desert Laboratory

28. Quoted in Hershberg, *James B. Conant*, p. 166.

29. Quoted in Nuel Pharr Davis, *Lawrence and Oppenheimer*. New York: Simon and Schuster, 1968, p. 143.

30. Quoted in Los Alamos National Laboratory (reprint), *Los Alamos, 1943–1945: The Beginning of an Era*. Los Alamos, NM: Los Alamos National Laboratory, 1984, p. 11.

31. Quoted in Los Alamos National Laboratory(reprint), *Los Alamos, 1943–1945*, p. 12.

32. Quoted in Miles O'Brien, "Special: Building the Bomb," CNN World News, October 2, 1995. http://cnn.com/WORLD/9508/Hiroshimabomb/index.html.

33. Quoted in Los Alamos National Laboratory (reprint), *Los Alamos, 1943-1945*, p. 12.

34. Quoted in Atomic Archive, "Reflections of the Nuclear Age."

35. Quoted in Atomic Archive, "Reflections of the Nuclear Age."

36. Quoted in Atomic Archive, "Reflections of the Nuclear Age."

Chapter 4: The Race Against Time

37. Quoted in Isidor Rabi et al., *Oppenheimer: The Story of One of the Most Remarkable Personalities of Our Time*. New York: Scribner's, 1969, p. 24.

38. *In the Matter of J. Robert Oppenheimer, Transcript of Hearings Before the U.S. Atomic Energy Commission*. Washington, DC: U.S. Government Printing Office, 1954, p. 31.

39. Quoted in Stephen Delaney Hale, "Young Men Served in Manhattan Project," *Augusta Chronicle*, February 8, 1999, p. 1.

40. Quoted in Hale, "Young Men Served in Manhattan Project," p. 1.

41. Compton, *Atomic Quest*, p. 212.

42. Fermi, *Atoms in the Family*, p. 205.

43. Quoted in James Gleick, *Genius: The Life and Science of Richard Feynman*. New York: Pantheon, 1992, p. 165.

44. Quoted in O'Brien, "Special."

Chapter 5: Will It Work?

45. Quoted in Robert James Maddox, "The Biggest Decision: Why We Had to Drop the Atomic Bomb," *American Heritage*, May/June 1995, p. 72.

46. Quoted in Maddox, "The Biggest Decision," p. 72.

47. Quoted in Compton, *Atomic Quest*, p. 247.

48. Quoted in Ferenc Szasz, *The Day the Sun Rose Twice*. Albuquerque: University of New Mexico Press, 1984, p. 81.

49. Leslie R. Groves, *Now It Can Be Told*. New York: Harper, 1962, p. 296.

50. Quoted in Bill Dietrich, "Fifty Years from Trinity," part 1, *Seattle Times*, 1995. www.seattletimes.com/trinity/articles/part1.html.

51. Quoted in O'Brien, "Special."

52. Quoted in Anthony Cave Brown and Charles B. MacDonald, *The Secret History of the Atomic Bomb*. New York: Dell, 1977, p. 516.

53. Quoted in Brown and MacDonald, *The Secret History of the Atomic Bomb*, p. 516.

54. Quoted in U.S. National Archives, "Trinity Test, July 16, 1945, Eyewitness Accounts," Record Group 227, OSRD-S1 Committee, box 82, folder 6, "Trinity."

55. Enrico Fermi, "My Observations During the Explosion at Trinity on July 16, 1945," Atomic Archive. www.atomicarchive.com/Docs/Fermi.shtml.

56. Groves, *Now It Can Be Told*, p. 296.

57. Robert Serber, "Eyewitness Accounts of the Explosion at Trinity on July 16, 1945," Atomic Archive. www.atomicarchive.com/Docs/Serber.shtml.

58. Serber, "Eyewitness Accounts of the Explosion at Trinity on July 16, 1945."

59. Quoted in Atomic Archive, "Reflections of the Nuclear Age."

60. Quoted in Atomic Archive, "Reflections of the Nuclear Age."

61. Quoted in Kurzman, *Day of the Bomb*, p. 361.

62. Quoted in James W. Kunetka, *City of Fire: Los Alamos and the Atomic Age, 1943–1945*. Albuquerque: University of New Mexico Press, 1978, p. 170.

63. Quoted in U.S. National Archives, "Trinity Test."

64. Quoted in Los Alamos National Laboratory (reprint), *Los Alamos, 1943–1945*, p. 57.

Chapter 6: Momentous Decisions

65. Quoted in Kurzman, *Day of the Bomb*, p. 363.

66. Quoted in Kurzman, *Day of the Bomb*, p. 365.

67. Harry S. Truman, *Memoirs by Harry S. Truman 1945: Year of Decisions*. Garden City, NY: Doubleday, 1955, p. 416.

68. Quoted in Richard Rhodes, *The Making of the Atomic Bomb*. New York: Simon and Schuster, 1987, p. 154.

69. Quoted in John Toland, *The Rising Sun: The Decline and Fall of the Japanese Empire, 1936–1945*. New York: Random House, 1970, p. 222.

70. Scientific Panel of the Interim Committee on Nuclear Power, "Recommendations on the Immediate Use of Nuclear Weapons," June 16, 1945, U.S. National Archives, Record Group 77, Records of the Office of the Chief of Engineers, Manhattan Engineer District, Harrison-Bundy File, folder 76.

71. Quoted in *Dictionary of Scientific Biography*, vol. 10. New York: Scribner's, 1971, p. 216.

72. Compton, *Atomic Quest*, p. 247.

73. Quoted in Atomic Archive, "Reflections of the Nuclear Age."

74. Winston Churchill and John Keegan, *Triumph and Tragedy: The Second World War*. Boston: Houghton Mifflin, 1986, p. 553.

75. Quoted in Herbert Feis, *The Atomic Bomb and the End of World War II*. Princeton, NJ: Princeton University Press, 1966, p. 55.

76. Quoted in Gar Aperovitz, *The Decision to Use the Atomic Bomb and the Architecture of an American Myth*. New York: Knopf, 1995, p. 353.

77. Quoted in Aperovitz, *The Decision to Use the Atomic Bomb and the Architecture of an American Myth*, p. 354.

78. Quoted in Robert H. Ferrell, *Off the Record: The Private Papers of Harry S. Truman*. New York: Harper and Row, 1980, pp. 55–56.

79. Truman, *Memoirs*, pp. 419–20.

80. Official Bombing Order, July 25, 1945, U.S. National Archives, Record Group 77, Records of the Office of the Chief of Engineers, Manhattan Engineer District, TS Manhattan Project File '42 to '45, folder 5B.

81. Quoted in Kurzman, *Day of the Bomb*, p. 394.

82. Hiroko Nakamoto and M. M. Pace, *My Japan: 1930–51*. New York: McGraw-Hill, 1970, pp. 21–22.

83. Quoted in Kurzman, *Day of the Bomb*, pp. 390–91.

84. Quoted in John R. Roberson, *Japan: From Shogun to SONY: 1543 to 1984*. New York: Atheneum, 1985, p. 54.

85. Quoted in Kurzman, *Day of the Bomb*, p. 408.

86. Quoted in Kurzman, *Day of the Bomb*, p. 408.

Chapter 7: "What Have We Done?"

87. Quoted in Gordon Thomas and Max Morgan Witts, *Enola Gay*. New York: Stein and Day, 1977, p. 239.

88. Quoted in Thomas and Witts, *Enola Gay*, p. 240.

89. Quoted in Thomas and Witts, *Enola Gay*, p. 250.

90. Quoted in Thomas and Witts, *Enola Gay*, pp. 252–53.

91. Quoted in Thomas and Witts, *Enola Gay*, p. 256.

92. Quoted in Evan Thomas, "Why We Did

It," *Newsweek,* July 24, 1995, p. 21.

93. Quoted in Thomas, "Why We Did It," p. 21.

94. Quoted in Thomas, "Why We Did It," p. 21.

95. Quoted in Thomas, "Why We Did It," p. 25.

96. Quoted in Hiroshima Peace Cultural Center and NHK, "Voice of Hibakusha: Hiroshima Witness." http://www.lclark.edu/~history/HIROSHIMA/dirc-litr.html.

97. Quoted in Hiroshima Peace Cultural Center and NHK, "Voice of Hibakusha."

98. Quoted in Sally MacDonald, "Hiroshima Memories: Fifty Years from Trinity," part 2, *Seattle Times,* 1995. www.seattletimes.com/trinity/supplement/hiroshima.html.

99. Quoted in Hiroshima Peace Cultural Center and NHK, "Voice of Hibakusha."

100. Quoted in ThinkQuest Team 20920, "Reports of Survivors," *The History and Making of the Atomic Bomb.* http://library.advanced.org/20920/survivors.html.

101. Quoted in Rhodes, *The Making of the Atomic Bomb,* p. 724.

102. Quoted in Thomas and Witts, *Enola Gay,* p. 268.

103. Quoted in Los Alamos National Laboratory (reprint), *Los Alamos, 1943–1945,* p. 60.

104. Quoted in Los Alamos National Laboratory (reprint), *Los Alamos, 1943–1945,* p. 60.

105. David McCullough, *Truman.* New York: Simon and Schuster, 1992, p. 455.

106. *Public Papers of the Presidents of the United States: Harry S. Truman, Containing the Public Messages, Speeches, and Statements of the President, April 12 to December 31, 1945.* Washington, DC: U.S. Government Printing Office, 1961, p. 212.

107. Quoted in C. V. Glines, "The Bomb That Ended World War II," *Aviation History Magazine,* January 1997, p. 3.

108. Quoted in Frank W. Chinnock, *Nagasaki: The Forgotten Bomb.* New York: World, 1969, p. 14.

109. Quoted in Glines, "The Bomb That Ended World War II," p. 2.

110. Quoted in Chinnock, *Nagasaki,* p. 140.

111. Quoted in Chinnock, *Nagasaki,* p. 142.

112. Quoted in Roberson, *Japan,* pp. 160–61.

113. Quoted in Glines, "The Bomb That Ended World War II," p. 2.

114. Quoted in Roberson, *Japan,* pp. 160-61.

Chapter 8: Where Next?

115. Quoted in Peter Goodchild, *J. Robert Oppenheimer: Shatterer of Worlds.* New York: Fromm International, 1985, p. 172.

116. Quoted in Richard N. Current et al., eds., *Words That Made American History.* Boston: Little, Brown, 1972, p. 47.

117. Harry S. Truman, "Statement Announcing the First Soviet A-Bomb—1949," Atomic Archive, May 16, 1999. www.atomic archive.com/Docs/SovietAB.shtml.

118. Quoted in John Hersey, *Hiroshima.* New York: Knopf, 1988, pp. 177–78.

119. Albert Einstein, *Ideas and Opinions.* New York: Wings Books, 1954, p. 115.

120. Einstein, *Ideas and Opinions,* pp. 115–16.

121. Compton, *Atomic Quest,* p. 299.

122. Hans Bethe, "An Open Letter from Hans Bethe," 1994. www.haverford.edu/math/davidon/hans_bethe.html.

123. Quoted in Rhodes, *The Making of the Atomic Bomb,* p. 770.

124. Quoted in Szasz, *The Day the Sun Rose Twice,* p. 89.

125. Quoted in O'Brien, "Special."

126. Quoted in Oak Ridge National Laboratory, "Scientists and Second Thoughts," June 8, 1994. www.ornl.gov/swords/secondthoughts.html.

127. Quoted in Chinnock, *Nagasaki,* p. 296.

For Further Reading

Necia H. Apfel, *It's All Relative: Einstein's Theory of Relativity*. New York: Lothrop, Lee, and Shepard, 1981. Using diagrams and photographs, the author explains the basic concepts of Einstein's famous theories.

Rodney Barker, *The Hiroshima Maidens*. New York: Viking, 1985. Experiences of bomb survivors who were brought to America to receive reconstructive surgery and vocational assistance. The author's family housed one of the young women during her stay in the United States.

Wallace B. Black and Jean F. Blashfield, *Hiroshima and the Atomic Bomb*. Glendale, CA: Crestwood House, 1993. Examines the decision leading to the use of the bomb, how the bomb affected the people involved, and the dawning of the atomic age.

Edward F. Dolan, *America in World War II: 1945*. Brookfield, CT: Millbrook, 1995. Account of the events in the United States during the last year of the war; discusses the lives of everyday citizens as well as government, industry, and the military.

Freeman Dyson, *Weapons and Hope*. New York: Harper and Row, 1984. A physicist explores the historical and cultural context in which nuclear arms were developed and offers solutions for avoiding future tragedies.

David E. Fisher, *The Ideas of Einstein*. New York: Holt, Rinehart, and Winston, 1980. Fisher describes Einstein's major theories in terms geared for younger readers.

Stephane Groueff, *Manhattan Project*. Boston: Little, Brown, 1967. Detailed account of the events that led to the building of the bombs, the decision to use them, and the aftermath.

David Halberstam, *The Fifties*. New York: Villard, 1993. Comprehensive look at American life during the 1950s; discusses cold war events and anti-Communist sentiments as well as fears of nuclear war.

Burt Hirschfeld, *Freedom in Jeopardy: The Story of the McCarthy Years*. New York: Julian Messner, 1969. A look at Senator Joseph McCarthy and other major figures involved in the anti-Communist crusade in the United States during the early 1950s.

Michael G. Kort, *The Cold War*. Brookfield, CT: Millbrook, 1993. Shows how the cold war evolved at the end of World War II and led to tense relations between the United States and the USSR and the nuclear arms race that continued for several decades.

Don Lawson, *The United States in World War II*. New York: Abelard-Schuman, 1963. Describes historical events of the war as well as daily life and the mood of the American people between 1941 and 1945.

Betty Jean Lifton, *A Place Called Hiroshima*. Tokyo: Kodansha International, 1985. Compassionate look at the experiences of the survivors of the bomb, describing their lives since August 6, 1945; shows development of a world peace movement in Hiroshima.

Thomas Parrish, *The Cold War Encyclopedia*. New York: Facts On File, 1996. Reference work on major people, places, events, and issues related to the cold war between the Communist bloc and Western Allies after World War II.

Marianne Philbin, ed., *The Ribbon: A Celebration of Life*. Asheville, NC: Lark Books, 1985. The story of the antiwar ribbon, constructed of cloth banners made by people around the world. On the fortieth anniversary of Hiroshima, thousands of people marched for peace and carried the banner around the U.S. Pentagon.

Victoria Sherrow, *Great Scientists*. New York: Facts On File, 1992. Profiles of Albert Einstein, Arthur Compton, Robert Oppenheimer, and Enrico Fermi show their scientific contributions to the development of nuclear energy and their lives after 1945.

R. Conrad Stein, *World War II in the Pacific*. Springfield, NJ: Enslow, 1994. Covers the events involving the war between Japan and the United States, from Pearl Harbor to the end of the war in 1945.

Richard Steins, *The Allies Against the Axis: World War II (1940–1950)*. New York: Twenty-First Century Books, 1994. A historical account of World War II between the United States and its European allies against Nazi Germany, Italy, and Japan; the book uses primary sources such as letters, diaries, speeches, and newspaper articles.

———, *The Postwar Years: The Cold War and Atomic Age (1950–1959)*. New York: Twenty-First Century Books, 1994. Description of life in the decade after the war, highlighting events in the cold war and nuclear arms race; uses primary sources such as letters, diaries, speeches, and newspaper articles.

Lisa Yount, *Contemporary Women Scientists*. New York: Facts On File, 1994. Profiles include Maria Goeppart Mayer, a physicist who worked on the Manhattan Project.

Works Consulted

Books

Michael Amrine, *Great Decision: The Secret History of the Atomic Bomb*. New York: Putnam, 1959. Analyzes the array of political, military, and humane considerations that went into the decision to use atomic bombs in 1945.

Gar Aperovitz, *The Decision to Use the Atomic Bomb and the Architecture of an American Myth*. New York: Knopf, 1995. Critical look at the political and military aspects of the decision to drop atomic weapons on Japan.

Kenneth T. Bainbridge, *Trinity*. Los Alamos, NM: Los Alamos Scientific Laboratory, (La-6300-H), 1946. Description of research leading to the first atomic test on July 16, 1945, by a leading British physicist who worked at Los Alamos.

Michael Barson, *Better Dead than Red*. New York: Hyperion, 1992. Ironic look at the cold war years; numerous illustrations include photos of famous people, posters, news headlines, political cartoons, and magazine ads selling fallout shelters.

Jeremy Bernstein, *Hans Bethe, Prophet of Energy*. New York: Basic Books, 1979. Comprehensive biography of the physicist who led the theoretical scientific unit at Los Alamos.

Hans Bethe, *The Road from Los Alamos*. New York: American Institute of Physics, 1991. Firsthand account by one of the leading theoretical physicists at Los Alamos.

Anthony Cave Brown and Charles B. MacDonald, *The Secret History of the Atomic Bomb*. New York: Dell, 1977. First-person accounts enliven this scientific, political, and military history of the atomic bomb project.

Grant Burns, *The Atomic Papers*. San Francisco: Scarecrow, 1984. Annotated bibliography of sources relating to the scientific and technological development of the bomb, the nuclear arms race, peacetime uses of nuclear power, and the peace movement.

James M. Burns, *Roosevelt: The Soldier of Freedom*. New York: Harcourt, Brace, 1970. Biography of President Franklin Roosevelt; discusses his wartime policies and decision to fund the bomb project.

Frank W. Chinnock, *Nagasaki: The Forgotten Bomb*. New York: World, 1969. A detailed account of the second atomic bomb ever used, the plutonium bomb that struck Nagasaki; includes first-person accounts from members of the bombing crew and from survivors.

Albert B. Christman and Al Christman, *Target Hiroshima: Deak Parsons and the Creation of the Atomic Bomb*. Annapolis, MD: United States Naval Institute, 1998. A biography of William "Deak"

Parsons, the scientist and naval officer who served as ordnance chief at Los Alamos and later assembled the bomb en route to Hiroshima.

Winston Churchill and John Keegan, *Triumph and Tragedy: The Second World War*. Boston: Houghton Mifflin, 1986.

Arthur Holly Compton, *Atomic Quest*. New York: Oxford University Press, 1956. First-person account of the bomb-building project by a Nobel Prize–winning physicist who helped to guide the project from beginning to end.

Richard N. Current et al., eds., *Words That Made American History*. Boston: Little, Brown, 1972. A collection of primary source materials, including newspaper articles, speeches, documents, and diaries.

Nuel Pharr Davis, *Lawrence and Oppenheimer*. New York: Simon and Schuster, 1968. Focuses on two of the major figures—physicists Ernest Lawrence and Robert Oppenheimer—involved in the Manhattan Project.

Dictionary of Scientific Biography. Vol. 10. New York: Scribner's, 1971. Includes profiles of major scientists involved in the bomb-building project.

Albert Einstein, *Ideas and Opinions*. New York: Wings Books, 1954.

Herbert Feis, *The Atomic Bomb and the End of World War II*. Princeton, NJ: Princeton University Press, 1966. Dramatic historical account of the race to build the bomb, the decision to use it, and the mission of the *Enola Gay*.

Laura Capon Fermi, *Atoms in the Family: My Life with Enrico Fermi*. Chicago: University of Chicago Press, 1954. The wife of Enrico Fermi, herself a scientist, writes about her husband's life and work, which included developing the atomic pile and then building the bombs themselves.

Robert H. Ferrell, *Off the Record: The Private Papers of Harry S. Truman*. New York: Harper and Row, 1980. Diaries, letters, and other papers show how Truman learned about the bomb and made the decision to use it.

Charles Frank, *Project Epsilon: The Farm Hall Transcripts*. Philadelphia: Institute of Physics, 1993. Fascinating inside look at the German bomb project as described by Werner Heisenberg and other German scientists who were sequestered in England after the Allies won the war in Europe; includes transcripts of secretly taped coversations that first became public in 1992.

John A. Garraty, *The American Nation: A History of the United States Since 1865*. New York: Harper & Row, 1979. American political and economic history from the Civil War to the late 1970s.

Len Giovannitti and Fred Freed, *The Decision to Drop the Bomb*. New York: Coward-McCann, 1965. Explores the people and issues surrounding the decision to use atomic weapons against the Japanese in 1945; firsthand accounts.

James Gleick, *Genius: The Life and Science of Richard Feynman.* New York: Pantheon, 1992. Biography of one of the leading scientists who worked at Los Alamos on the Manhattan Project.

Peter Goodchild, *J. Robert Oppenheimer: Shatterer of Worlds.* New York: Fromm International, 1985. Engrossing biography of the scientific director of the Manhattan Project.

Stephane Groueff, *Manhattan Project.* Boston: Little, Brown, 1967. Fascinating and detailed look at the people and events leading to the development of atomic weapons during World War II.

Leslie R. Groves, *Now It Can Be Told.* New York: Harper, 1962. The military director of the bomb project gives an inside view of the Manhattan Project, from its inception through the use of atomic weapons.

Michihiko Hachiya, *Hiroshima Diary.* Trans. W. Wells. Chapel Hill: University of North Carolina Press, 1969. A physician's compelling firsthand account of human experiences after the bomb struck Hiroshima.

Niels H. de V. Heathcote, *Breakthroughs in Twentieth Century Science: Nobel Prize Winners in Physics, 1901–1950.* New York: Henry Schuman, 1953. Profiles of Albert Einstein, Ernest Rutherford, Enrico Fermi, Niels Bohr, and other scientists whose discoveries laid the groundwork for nuclear energy and atomic weapons.

John Hersey, *Hiroshima.* New York: Knopf, 1988. Hersey's acclaimed book, based on extensive interviews, contains riveting accounts from atomic bomb survivors.

James Hershberg, *James B. Conant: Harvard to Hiroshima and Making of the Nuclear Age.* New York: Knopf, 1993. Detailed biography of scientist and university dean James B. Conant, who urged the U.S. government to begin atomic research in the 1930s and served as a key administrator throughout the bomb-building project.

James W. Kunetka, *City of Fire: Los Alamos and the Atomic Age, 1943–1945.* Albuquerque: University of New Mexico Press, 1978. Historical account of Project Y, the building and testing of atomic weapons at Los Alamos.

Dan Kurzman, *Day of the Bomb: Countdown to Hiroshima.* New York: McGraw-Hill, 1986. Explores the discoveries, projects, and decisions that led to the use of atomic weapons against Japan; author profiles key figures, such as Leo Szilard, Robert Oppenheimer, General Leslie Groves, Emperor Hirohito, and the spy Klaus Fuchs.

Lansing Lamont, *Day of Trinity.* New York: Atheneum, 1965. Lively historical account of the Manhattan Project. Author interviewed many nonscientists who worked at Los Alamos—including federal agents, guards, family members, and cooks—to get a unique perspective.

William Lanouette, *Genius in the Shadows: A Biography of Leo Szilard, the Man Be-*

hind the Bomb. Chicago: University of Chicago Press, 1994. Fascinating look at the brilliant scientist and inventor who may have been the first person to envision a nuclear chain reaction. Szilard spurred U.S. atomic research but opposed use of the bomb in 1945.

William L. Laurence, Dawn over Zero: The Story of the Atomic Bomb. New York: Knopf, 1947. Account of the Manhattan Project, Trinity test, and bombings of Japan as seen by the journalist who was chosen to witness secret events and later report on them.

Los Alamos National Laboratory (reprint), Los Alamos, 1943–1945: The Beginning of an Era. Los Alamos, NM: Los Alamos National Laboratory, 1984. Illustrated account of the bomb-building project at Los Alamos; covers scientific and technical aspects of design, production, and testing.

David McCullough, Truman. New York: Simon and Schuster, 1992. Comprehensive biography of the president who made the decision to use the bomb and helped to shape U.S. nuclear policy in the early cold war years.

Members of the Overseas Press Club of America, How I Got That Story. New York: E. P. Dutton, 1967. In "The Greatest Story," journalist William Laurence describes how he was chosen as the one reporter allowed to observe and write about the Manhattan Project and the bombings of Japan.

Takashi Nagai, We of Nagasaki: The Story of Survivors in an Atomic Wasteland. New York: Meredith, 1951. Firsthand accounts of the horrors of the bombing of Nagasaki in August 1945 and its aftermath.

Hiroko Nakamoto and M. M. Pace, My Japan: 1930–51. New York: McGraw-Hill, 1970. Life in Japan during and after World War II as experienced by ordinary people; vivid firsthand accounts show how young people survived these years.

Arata Osada, Children of the A-Bomb. Trans. Jean Dan and Ruth Sieben-Morgan. New York: Putnam, 1963. Heartrending firsthand accounts by young survivors of the Hiroshima and Nagasaki bombings; describes long-term effects of the bomb.

Isidor Rabi et al., Oppenheimer: The Story of One of the Most Remarkable Personalities of Our Time. New York: Scribner's, 1969. Biography of the man who directed the scientific aspects of the bomb project, written by his colleagues.

Richard Rhodes, The Making of the Atomic Bomb. New York: Simon and Schuster, 1987. An extensive Pulitzer Prize–winning account of the events that led to the creation of nuclear weapons and the bombings of two Japanese cities in 1945.

John R. Roberson, Japan: From Shogun to SONY: 1543 to 1984. New York: Atheneum, 1985. A readable history of Japan that covers the war years.

Stefan Rozental, Niels Bohr, His Life and Work as Seen by His Friends and Colleagues.

Amsterdam: North-Holland, 1985. Biography of the Nobel laureate whose research in nuclear physics laid the groundwork for the development of atomic energy.

Scott D. Sagan and Kenneth Waltz, *The Spread of Nuclear Weapons.* New York: W. W. Norton, 1995. Authors debate pros and cons of the proliferation of nuclear weapons and the possibilities that they might be used.

Ruth Lewin Sime, *Lise Meitner: A Life in Physics.* Berkeley and Los Angeles: University of California Press, 1996. Absorbing biography of the scientist who first used the term *nuclear fission* and carried out key research that led to the discovery of nuclear energy.

Alice Kimball Smith and Charles Weiner, eds., *Robert Oppenheimer: Letters and Recollections.* Cambridge, MA: Harvard University Press, 1980. Personal correspondence, documents, speeches, and other materials illuminate the life and work of physicist Robert Oppenheimer.

Charles W. Sweeney with James A. Antonucci and Marion K. Antonucci, *War's End: An Eyewitness Account of America's Last Atomic Mission.* New York: Hearst, 1997. Sweeney, the pilot of *Bock's Car* and a crew member of the *Enola Gay,* describes the rigorous training, planning, secrecy, and problems involved in the 1945 bombing missions.

Ferenc Szasz, *The Day the Sun Rose Twice.* Albuquerque: University of New Mexico Press, 1984. Detailed look at the events culminating in the world's first nuclear explosion on July 16, 1945.

Ronald Takaki, *Hiroshima.* Boston: Little, Brown, 1995. Takaki analyzes the political and social motives behind the use of the bomb and raises charges of anti-Japanese racism.

Gordon Thomas and Max Morgan Witts, *Enola Gay.* New York: Stein and Day, 1977. Vivid account of the top-secret bombing mission on August 6, 1945, based on interviews with the pilot and crew members of the *Enola Gay.*

Paul W. Tibbets, *Flight of the Enola Gay.* Reynoldsburg, OH: Buckeye Aviation Book, 1989. The *Enola Gay* commander recalls the events surrounding the flight that made history by dropping the first atomic bomb ever used in wartime.

———, *The Tibbets Story.* New York: Stein and Day, 1978. Autobiography of the pilot who commanded the secret bombing mission on Hiroshima and trained the crew members who carried out both atomic missions.

John Toland, *The Rising Sun: The Decline and Fall of the Japanese Empire, 1936–1945.* New York: Random House, 1970. Fascinating political, economic, and social history of the Japanese just before and during World War II.

Harry S. Truman, *Memoirs by Harry S. Truman 1945: Year of Decisions.* Garden City, NY: Doubleday, 1955. Truman's account of 1945, the year he became president upon Roosevelt's death and learned about the atomic bomb.

Mark Walker, *Nazi Science: Myth, Truth, and the German Atomic Bomb.* London: Plenum, 1995. A detailed look at atomic weapons research in Nazi Germany. Profiles key scientists and their efforts and includes materials that were first made public in 1992.

Robert C. Williams, *Klaus Fuchs, Atom Spy.* Cambridge, MA: Harvard University Press, 1987. Biography of the Austrian-born physicist who, while working at Los Alamos as part of the British team, gave atomic secrets to the Soviets.

Jane S. Wilson and Charlotte Serber, eds., *Standing By and Making Do: Women in Wartime Los Alamos.* Los Alamos, NM: Los Alamos Historical Society, 1988. First-person accounts enrich this history of the women who worked and lived at Los Alamos during the Manhattan Project.

Allan M. Winkler, *Life Under a Cloud.* New York: Oxford University Press, 1993. The author examines the social and emotional effects of life in the nuclear age.

Peter Wyden, *Day One: Before Hiroshima and After.* New York: Simon and Schuster, 1984. Engrossing account of the creation, testing, and dropping of nuclear weapons in 1945.

Periodicals

Harold Agnew, "Birth of an Atomic 'Little Boy,'" *Newsweek,* March 8, 1999. Reminiscences of one of the physicists who helped to build the atomic pile in Chicago, worked on the bomb at Los Alamos and on Tinian Island, and flew in a plane that accompanied the *Enola Gay* to Hiroshima.

Joseph Albright and Marcia Kunstel, "The Boy Who Gave Away the Bomb," *New York Times Magazine,* September 14, 1997. Profile and interview of Theodore Hall, who at age nineteen was the youngest scientist at Los Alamos, and his reasons for giving atomic secrets to Soviet agents during the war.

Economist, "Guilt, Shame, and Hiroshima," August 5, 1995. As new generations try to understand what happened, this article examines the controversy surrounding the decision to bomb Hiroshima with atomic weapons.

George Elsey, "The Russians Steal an Ally's Atomic Secrets," *Newsweek,* March 8, 1999. Elsey, an aide to President Truman, shares his recollections of the Potsdam meeting.

C. V. Glines, "The Bomb That Ended World War II," *Aviation History Magazine,* January 1997. Fascinating details about the problem-riddled flight of *Bock's Car,* which dropped the atomic bomb on Nagasaki, Japan.

Stephen Delaney Hale, "Young Men Served in Manhattan Project," *Augusta Chronicle,* February 8, 1999.

Caroline L. Herzenberg and Ruth H. Howes, "Women of the Manhattan

Project," *Technology Review,* November/December 1993. Describes contributions made by female physicists, mathematicians, engineers, and others working on all phases of the project; discusses discrimination against female scientists during and after the war.

Robert James Maddox, "The Biggest Decision: Why We Had to Drop the Atomic Bomb," *American Heritage,* May/June 1995. Discusses why Truman and his advisers believed the bomb was the best way to end the war and save lives in the long run.

A. M. Rosenthal, "A Return to Hiroshima," *New York Times,* August 1995. Editorial discusses historic context surrounding the decision to use nuclear bombs on Japan.

John P. Sullivan, "Surrender at Sea," *Newsweek,* March 8, 1999. Recollections of a seaman who witnessed the Japanese surrender on September 2, 1945, aboard the USS *Missouri.*

Evan Thomas, "Why We Did It," *Newsweek,* July 24, 1995. A discussion about whether the United States should have dropped atomic bombs on Japan.

Shizuko Yamasaki, "At Ground Zero in Hiroshima," *Newsweek,* March 8, 1999. Victim of the bombing describes the horrors she and her young son endured during and after the bombing.

Documents

Corbin Allardice and Edward R. Trapnell, "The First Atomic Pile: An Eyewitness Account Revealed by Some of the Participants and Narratively Recorded." Washington, DC: U.S. Atomic Energy Commission, November 1949.

Albert Einstein, "Letter to President Roosevelt," Public Record, Argonne National Laboratory.

In the Matter of J. Robert Oppenheimer, Transcript of Hearings Before the U.S. Atomic Energy Commission. Washington, DC: U.S. Government Printing Office, 1954.

Official Bombing Order, July 25, 1945, U.S. National Archives, Record Group 77, Records of the Office of the Chief of Engineers, Manhattan Engineer District, TS Manhattan Project File '42 to '45, folder 5B.

Public Papers of the Presidents of the United States: Harry S. Truman, Containing the Public Messages, Speeches, and Statements of the President, April 12 to December 31, 1945. Washington, DC: U.S. Government Printing Office, 1961.

Scientific Panel of the Interim Committee on Nuclear Power, "Recommendations on the Immediate Use of Nuclear Weapons," June 16, 1945, U.S. National Archives, Record Group 77, Records of the Office of the Chief of Engineers, Manhattan Engineer District, Harrison-Bundy File, folder 76.

U.S. National Archives, "Trinity Test, July 16, 1945, Eyewitness Accounts," Record Group 227, OSRD-S1 Committee, box 82, folder 6, "Trinity."

Internet Sources

Argonne National Laboratory, "The 'Last Universal Scientist' Takes Charge," *Frontiers*, 1996. www.anl.gov/OPA/frontiers96 unisci.html.

———, "Piglet and the Pumpkin Field," *Frontiers*, 1996. www.anl.gov.80/OPA/frontiers96/piglet.html.

Atomic Archive, "Reflections of the Nuclear Age." http://atomicarchive.com//AAReflection.shtml.

Hans Bethe, "An Open Letter from Hans Bethe," 1994. www.haverford.edu/math/davidon/hans_bethe.html.

John T. Correll, "The Decision That Launched the Enola Gay." www.afa.org/enolagay/03-02.html.

Bill Dietrich, "Fifty Years from Trinity," part 1, *Seattle Times*, 1995. www.seattletimes.com/trinity/articles/part1.html.

Enola Gay, "Statement Offered by Brigadier General Paul W. Tibbets (USAF-Retired) at the Airmen Memorial Museum on June 8, 1994." www.theenolagay.com/plane.htm.

Enrico Fermi, "My Observations During the Explosion at Trinity on July 16, 1945," Atomic Archive. www.atomicarchive.com/Docs/Fermi.shtml.

Bill Goodman, "WWII Story: This Is It," All Aviation Flight OnLine. http://aafo.com/library/history/B17/b17part3.htm.

Hiroshima Peace Cultural Center and NHK, "Voices of Hibakusha: Hiroshima Witness." http://www.lclark, edu/~history/HIROSHIMA/dirc-litr.html.

Sally MacDonald, "Hiroshima Memories: Fifty Years from Trinity," part 2, *Seattle Times*, 1995. www.seattletimes.com/trinity/supplement/hiroshima.html

Lance Morrow, "Hiroshima and the Time Machine," *Time*, September 19, 1994. http://cgi.pathfinder.com/time/magazine/archive/1994/940919/940919.essay.html.

Oak Ridge National Laboratory, "The Forties: War and Peace." www.ornl.gov/swords/forties.html.

———, "Scientists and Second Thoughts," June 8, 1994. www.ornl.gov/swords/second-thoughts.html.

Miles O'Brien, "Special: Building the Bomb," CNN World News, October 2, 1995. http://cnn.com/WORLD/9508/Hiroshimabomb/index.html.

Alex Roland, "Keep the Bomb," *TechReview*, August 1995. www.techreview.com/articles/aug95/AtomicRoland.html.

Richard Rhodes, "Atomic Physicist," *Time* (Scientists and Thinkers of the Twentieth Century), March 29, 1999. http://cgi.pathfinder.com/time/time100/scientist/index.html.

Robert Serber, "Eyewitness Accounts of the Explosion at Trinity on July 16, 1945," Atomic Archive. www.atomicarchive.com/Docs/Serber.shtml.

ThinkQuest Team 20920, *The History and Making of the Atomic Bomb*. http://library.advanced.org/20920.

Harry S. Truman, "Statement Announcing the First Soviet A-Bomb—1949," Atomic Archive, May 16, 1999. www.atomicarchive.com/Docs/SovietAB.shtml.

USS Indianapolis, "A Survivor's Story." www.indianapolis.org/woody/htm.

Websites

A-Bomb WWW Museum (www.csi.ad.jp/ABOMB). Contains facts and statistics, photographs, exhibits, essays, and first-person accounts of the bombing; information about the Hiroshima Peace Cultural Center.

Argonne National Laboratory (www.anl.gov/). Includes history of the S-1 project at the University of Chicago and the continuing nuclear research conducted at Argonne for peacetime purposes.

Atomic Archive (www.atomicarchive.com). Documents, letters, articles, and commentary relating to the Manhattan Project, bombings of Hiroshima and Nagasaki, and the postwar nuclear arms race.

Enola Gay (www.theenolagay.com/plane.htm). Material about the bombing mission, crews, and aircraft.

Hanford National Laboratory (www.hanford.gov/). Historical materials about the wartime production of plutonium and postwar research and development.

Oak Ridge National Laboratory (www.ornl.gov/). Historical materials relating to production of fissionable materials during the war and the postwar work at Oak Ridge.

Smithsonian Institution: Enola Gay exhibit (www.afa.org/enolagay/03-02.html). The institution's *Enola Gay* exhibit includes papers and documents highlighting the description of the Manhattan Project and the bombings.

Leo Szilard Home Page. (www.peak.org/). Includes letters, photographs, and documents relating to the development of atomic weapons and their use in 1945. Material on Leo Szilard includes his efforts to prevent the bombs from being used.

Index

Picture Credits

Cover photo: Corbis-Bettmann

AP/Wide World Photos, 23, 36 (left), 42, 49, 59, 63

Archive Photos, 20, 28, 35, 36 (right), 68

Corbis, 11, 15 (right), 16, 30, 31, 40, 47, 50, 53 (both), 70, 83, 84, 92, 96 (both), 98, 101, 103

Corbis/Horace Bristol, 38

Corbis/Historical Picture Archive, 64

Corbis/Hulton-Deutsch Collection, 25, 26, 39

Corbis/Reuters Newsmedia, Inc., 104

Corbis/David Samuel Robbins, 97

Corbis/Arthur Rothstein, 13

Corbis/Underwood & Underwood, 90

Corbis/Oscar White, 19

Corbis-Bettmann, 8, 10, 21, 32, 48, 55 (right), 62, 74, 77, 82 (bottom), 93, 95

Digital Stock, 27, 55 (left), 58, 73

FPG International, 44

Library of Congress, 14

Los Alamos National Laboratory, 34, 43, 46, 51, 61, 80, 85

National Archives, 67, 82 (top), 87

Martha Schierholz, 15 (left), 17, 24

Smithsonian Institution, 52, 69, 71, 75, 79, 91

Truman Library, 57

About the Author

Victoria Sherrow holds B.S. and M.S. degrees from Ohio State University. Among her writing credits are numerous stories and articles, six books of fiction, and more than forty works of nonfiction for children and young adults. Her recent books have explored such topics as biomedical ethics, the Great Depression, and the Holocaust. For Lucent Books, she has written *The Titanic, Life During the Gold Rush*, and *The Righteous Gentiles*. Sherrow lives in Connecticut with her husband, Peter Karoczkai, and their three children.

14473